Erwin Dee Kord (Ed.)

Penumbra: Overture

Erwin Dee Kord (Ed.)

Penumbra: Overture

Frictional Games, Single-Player Video Game

Solv

Contents

Articles

References

Penumbra: Overture

<table>
<tr><td colspan="2" align="center">Penumbra: Overture</td></tr>
<tr><td>Developer(s)</td><td>Frictional Games</td></tr>
<tr><td>Publisher(s)</td><td>Paradox Interactive</td></tr>
<tr><td>Designer(s)</td><td>Thomas Grip
Jens Nilsson
Tom Jubert</td></tr>
<tr><td>Composer(s)</td><td>Mikko Tarmia</td></tr>
<tr><td>Series</td><td>Penumbra</td></tr>
<tr><td>Engine</td><td>HPL</td></tr>
<tr><td>Version</td><td>1.1 [1] [2] [3]</td></tr>
<tr><td>Platform(s)</td><td>Microsoft Windows, Linux, Mac OS X</td></tr>
<tr><td>Release date(s)</td><td>Microsoft Windows
March 30, 2007
Linux:
May 25, 2007
Mac OS X:
January 10, 2008
Steam:
March 7, 2009</td></tr>
<tr><td>Genre(s)</td><td>Graphic adventure, Survival horror</td></tr>
<tr><td>Mode(s)</td><td>Single-player</td></tr>
<tr><td>Rating(s)</td><td>• ESRB: M
• PEGI: 12+</td></tr>
<tr><td>Media/distribution</td><td>DVD, Digital Download</td></tr>
</table>

Penumbra: Overture is the first in a series of episodic first-person adventure games developed by Swedish developer Frictional Games.[4] It was originally intended as the first episode of a trilogy. With the announcement of the second episode, *Penumbra: Black Plague*, it was stated that the second game would be the final chapter.[5] However, an expansion has been released since then: *Penumbra: Requiem*, technically giving the series a third chapter.[6]

Gameplay

Although Frictional Games describes *Penumbra: Overture* as a first-person adventure,[7] the game blends the genres of survival horror, first-person shooter and adventure. The use of Newton Game Dynamics emphasizes physics-based puzzles as well as physics-based combat.[8] The game also takes advantage of advanced artificial intelligence to respond realistically to noises and light, creating stealth-based gameplay. There are no firearms in the game, so during combat the player is limited to improvised melee fighting with a hammer or pickaxe,[9] or throwing objects at attacking creatures. The game is designed to emphasize stealth and avoidance over direct conflict. For example, Philip can close doors behind him to temporarily hold off attacking enemies.[10]

Opening a chest using the physics code

The game's main focus is on exploration and classic adventure game object interaction: examining and collecting objects and using them to solve puzzles.[11] These mostly involve finding keys or other objects that can either be used by themselves or in combination with each other to solve certain problems. In addition to these standard inventory based puzzles, *Overture* also offers several physics based puzzles where certain objects must be moved or manipulated in real time. Environmental objects such as doors, desk drawers, and switches on machinery must be opened or manipulated using realistic movements mirroring their use in the real world, and certain obstructions can only be cleared by utilizing certain objects in a specific way; for example, in order to solve one of the games puzzles a player may choose to stack boxes and barrels in such a manner as to allow for the player to be able to leap past an obstacle, such as an electrical fence, or to reach a certain area normally too high to reach.

Essential to puzzle solving is the ability to read written notes scattered around the mine by its previous inhabitants, which often offer clues or solutions as to how to get past a certain area, as well as providing plot exposition and character development. The player also has access to a notebook where important information is recorded and the players goals and objectives are recorded.

Story

Set in the year 2000, *Penumbra: Overture* follows the story of Philip, a thirty-year-old physicist whose mother recently died. After receiving a mysterious letter from his supposedly dead father, Philip follows a series of clues that lead to him to a mysterious location in uninhabited northern Greenland.[12] The harsh cold forces him to take shelter in an abandoned mine. Unfortunately, the mine's entrance collapses as he enters it, and he is forced to move deeper inside. Within the mine, Philip discovers diary extracts written by a scientist of some sort, who was alone and gradually resorted to eating cave-dwelling spiders as an alternative food source as his supplies diminished.

The unknown person also describes discovering a psychoactive toxin in the spiders and deduced that, after eight months of consuming them in the mine, it was beginning to have an effect on him, physically. Philip also begins receiving radio messages from Tom "Red" Redwood, a man driven insane by cabin fever. Red promises that if he is found, he will give Philip answers. The game follows Philip as he descends deeper into the mines in search of Red while unravelling the secrets of the mine's previous and current inhabitants.

Philip quickly discovers that the mine is inhabited by an ecosystem of abnormally large and hostile animals: dogs, giant spiders, and gargantuan earthworms among others. Abandoned outposts and various scattered papers found throughout the mine indicate that a secret society is studying some unusual phenomena inside the mines.

Following clues and solving various puzzles, Philip eventually comes to an area deep within the mine where Red is waiting for him. Red waits inside an incinerator where he begs Philip to kill him. With no other option, Philip activates the incinerator and amongst Red's remains, he finds items he needs to progress into a new area of the mine which is identified as "The Shelter". Once inside, Philip notices what appears to be a human watching him. Philip approaches the figure, but the lighting is suddenly extinguished and Philip is knocked out and dragged away.

Development

Tech demo

Penumbra: Overture is based on Frictional Games' earlier game *Penumbra*, a short tech demo meant to demonstrate the capabilities of the company's HPL Engine.

The developers admitted to making significant modifications of the original engine to accommodate the 3D graphics in this game, "The engine is built from an engine created when making a thesis job which resulted in the platform game Energetic. Before moving into the 3rd dimension I made some cleanup of the engine (which was quite rushed in some places) and started to add a base for 3D rendering. I would not say that the original 2D engine was modified to add 3D, but rather a 3D layer was added so all of the 2D stuff is still there. It is still possible to make a 2D tile game using our engine."[13]

The *Penumbra* Tech Demo from 2006

While not initially intended to be a commercial product, *Penumbra* was received exceedingly well, and Frictional decided to develop it into a full-length game.[7]

Release

The first episode of *Penumbra* was released on March 30, 2007, through various online distribution websites. The game was simultaneously released in a boxed edition in the United Kingdom, and

The full commercial game *Overture*

the boxed release in the United States was shipped to retailers on May 8, 2007.[14] On May 25, 2007, the full version for Linux was released on the Frictional Games store.

In addition, the game became available on GameTap on October 4, 2007. On January 10, 2008, the full version for Mac OS X was released on the Frictional Games forum for PowerPC and Intel architectures.[15] On March 6, 2009, Paradox Interactive released *Penumbra Overture* in a collection pack along with *Penumbra: Black Plague* and *Penumbra: Requiem*. The game became available via Steam on March 7, 2009.

Overture was released as part of the Humble Indie Bundle,[16] and when the Bundle made more than $1 million, *Overture's* source code was released as open source.[17] Frictional Games also hosts a dedicated forum on their website where people can discuss the code and any projects based around it.[18]

Reception

Reception	
Aggregate scores	
Aggregator	**Score**
GameRankings	73.74%[19] (PC)
Metacritic	73%[20] (PC)
Review scores	
Publication	**Score**
Adventure Gamers	★ ★ ★ ★ ★ [21]
Eurogamer	7.7/10[22] (PC)
GameSpot	7.8/10[23]
Adrenaline Vault	★ ★ ★ ★ ★ [24]
Worth Playing	★ ★ ★ ★ ★ ★ ★ ★ ★ ★ [25]
GameZone	★ ★ ★ ★ ★ ★ ★ ★ ★ ★ [26]

As of July 2011, the game has a MetaCritic score of 73,[20] a MobyGames rank of 74,[27] and a GameRankings rank of 73.74%,[19] as well as an average rating of four stars on the The Linux Game Tome[28] and average of four and a half stars at JeuxLinux.[29]

While the game received mostly favorable reviews, it was criticized on a number of fronts, especially for its rather crude combat system and sometimes confusing or poorly implemented story elements, causing Eurogamer to comment that the game would "do better if it relied on its own inherent spookiness rather than trying to create artificial atmosphere by banging on about a character we don't have any real reason to care about, something about his dad, destiny and miners writing stupidly long notes to themselves about their imminent horrible deaths." It did however praise the character of Red, stating that he was "the most compelling element of the narrative, and wonderfully acted."[22] GameSpot in its review commented on the combat by saying that fights are often "so frenetic that it's almost impossible to control your movements" and that "it would have been much more sensible for the camera to lock on and move with enemies." It did however note that it did help differentiate *Overture* from more action oriented titles, saying that the "end result of the difficult combat is that you feel like an average Joe who wants to avoid zombie dogs with glowing eyes, not a video game superman out to stack dead canines like cordwood."[23]

Despite these apparent flaws, the game was praised for its unsettling and creepy atmosphere, with Adrenaline Vault deciding that "every element in the game is geared to set a dark, scary mood. On occasion, you'll feel helpless, overwhelmed, guilty and frightened. I think this is helped, rather than hindered, by the developer's choice to keep physical fights intermittent and less gory and bloody than in many other horror games. The result is a sense of depressing solitude, with the disturbing knowledge that you're not alone."[24] The games approach to puzzle solving was also generally well received, with Worth Playing stating that "the control scheme adds an interesting touch to the game and helps with the immersion",[25] although GameZone in their review of the game complained that "sometimes having to interact with things in this way lead to problems, as in when necessary actions were hard to accomplish."[26] And while the games production values were lower than some of the other titles released around the same time, Adventure Gamers noted that for "an independent project from a team of four people, the game looks great, besides a few shoddy textures", and saying that the game's sound effects "help set the mood" and are "realistic and jarring".[21]

Many of the criticisms directed at *Overture* were taken into consideration during the development of the next episode *Penumbra: Black Plague*. These changes included the removal of dogs and other combat related enemies, as well as moving away somewhat from a reliance on written notes. The combat system was also dropped entirely and the physics system somewhat reworked, leading the game to be even more stealth based than its predecessor.[30] *Black Plague* received slightly more positive reviews from critics, and its design was for the most part mirrored with only a few additions by Frictional's critically acclaimed 2010 spiritual successor to the series *Amnesia: The Dark Descent.*

References

[1] "Frictional Games Support / Update 1.1 - April 22, 2010 - Penumbra: Overture" (http://support.frictionalgames.com/entry/77/). Support.frictionalgames.com. . Retrieved 2011-08-11.

[2] "Frictional Games Support / Linux - April 21, 2010 - 1.1 update for Penumbra Overture Linux" (http://support.frictionalgames.com/entry/65/). Support.frictionalgames.com. . Retrieved 2011-08-11.

[3] "Frictional Games Support / Mac - March 26, 2010 - 1.1 Mac Overture update" (http://support.frictionalgames.com/entry/79/). Support.frictionalgames.com. . Retrieved 2011-08-11.

[4] Paradox Interactive - Penumbra: Overture premieres game on Gamer's Gate (http://www.paradoxplaza.com/index. php?option=com_content&task=view&id=144&Itemid=129)

[5] "Penumbra to spread to computers again next year" (http://www.adventuregamers.com/newsitem.php?id=1527). Adventuregamers.com. 2007-09-13. . Retrieved 2007-09-20.

[6] News article from Gameplayer.se (swedish) (http://gameplayer.se/news.php?pub_id=10663)

[7] Penumbra: Overture (http://penumbra-overture.com/game.php)

[8] Penumbra Horror Games Overture, Black Plague, and Requiem Ported to Linux (http://linux.about.com/b/2009/07/18/penumbra-horror-games-overture-black-plague-and-requiem-ported-to-linux.htm) About.com, July 18, 2009

[9] Hands-on Penumbra Overture - PC (http://gaming.hexus.net/content/item.php?item=7698&page=1) HEXUS, January 19, 2007 (Article Steven Williamson)

[10] Indie horror adventure Penumbra: Overture available on Linux, coming to Mac (http://www.joystiq.com/2007/05/31/indie-horror-adventure-penumbra-on-linux-coming-to-mac/) Joystiq, May 31, 2007

[11] Penumbra Linux Release (http://www.escapistmagazine.com/news/view/72315-Penumbra-Linux-Release) The Escapist, May 31, 2007

[12] Penumbra Overture - If You Dare (http://www.tuxmachines.org/node/28379) tuxmachines.org, June 5, 2008

[13] Jens Nilsson, Thomas Grip, TJ Jubert - Frictional Games (http://www.adventureclassicgaming.com/index.php/site/interviews/293/) Adventure Classic Gaming, December 205, 2007 (Article by Philip Jong)

[14] Penumbra: Overture: FAQ (http://www.gotgameentertainment.com/penumbra/faq.htm)

[15] 2008-01 Thursday 10th, Penumbra: Overture released for Mac OS X! (http://www.frictionalgames.com/forum/thread-1492.html)

[16] Interview With Frictional Games – Penumbra/Amnesia (Tgdb.nl) (http://www.tgdb.nl/computer/specials/8614-interview-frictional-games.html)

[17] "The Humble Indie Bundle #3 (pay what you want for five awesome indie games)" (http://www.wolfire.com/humble). Wolfire.com. . Retrieved 2011-08-11.

[18] "Penumbra: Overture Game And Engine Source Code Released For Free" (http://www.megagames.com/news/penumbra-overture-game-and-engine-source-code-released-free). MegaGames. 2010-05-14. . Retrieved 2011-07-19.

[19] "*Penumbra: Overture* for PC" (http://www.gamerankings.com/pc/934076-penumbra-overture-episode-one/index.html). GameRankings. . Retrieved 2011-07-12.

[20] "*Penumbra: Overture* (PC): Reviews" (http://www.metacritic.com/game/pc/penumbra-overture). Metacritic. . Retrieved 2011-07-12.

[21] Boosinger, Austin (2007-05-15). "REVIEW: Penumbra: Overture" (http://www.adventuregamers.com/article/id,741/). Adventure Gamers. . Retrieved 2011-07-12.

[22] Meer, Alec (2007-03-30). "Penumbra: Overture - Review" (http://www.eurogamer.net/articles/penumbra-overture-review). Eurogamer. . Retrieved 2011-07-12.

[23] Todd, Brett (2007-05-04). "Penumbra: Overture Review" (http://www.gamespot.com/pc/action/penumbra/review.html). GameSpot. . Retrieved 2011-07-12. (PC)

[24] Mandel, Bob (2007-06-18). "Penumbra: Overture PC review" (http://www.avault.com/reviews/pc/review-of-penumbra-overture-episode-one/). Adrenaline Vault. . Retrieved 2011-07-12.

[25] King, James (2007-05-18). "PC Review - 'Penumbra: Overture'" (http://worthplaying.com/article/2007/5/18/reviews/42108/). Worth Playing. . Retrieved 2011-07-12.

[26] "Penumbra: Overture - PC - Review" (http://pc.gamezone.com/reviews/item/penumbra_overture_pc_review). GameZone. 2007-05-10. . Retrieved 2011-07-12.

[27] Penumbra: Overture at MobyGames (http://www.mobygames.com/game/penumbra-overture-episode-1)

[28] Penumbra: Overture Episode 1, The Linux Game Tome (http://happypenguin.org/show?Penumbra: Overture Episode 1)

[29] Penumbra: Overture - Game Profile (http://www.jeuxlinux.fr/spip.php?article118) JeuxLinux (French)

[30] RPS Interview: Penumbra's Tom Jubert (http://www.rockpapershotgun.com/2008/07/21/rps-interview-penumbras-tom-jubert/) Rock, Paper Shotgun, July 2, 2008 (Article by John Walker)

External links

- Official website (http://http://www.penumbra-overture.com)
- Original Penumbra tech demo (http://www.frictionalgames.com/site/penumbradownload/)
- Penumbra's github repository (https://github.com/FrictionalGames)

Graphic adventure game

A **graphic adventure game** is a form of adventure game.[1] They are distinct from text adventures. Whereas a player must actively observe using commands such as "look" in a text-based adventure, graphic adventures revolutionized gameplay by making use of natural human perception. Eventually, the text parser interface associated with older adventure games was phased out in favor of a point-and-click interface, i.e., a game where the player interacts with the game environment and objects using an on-screen cursor. In many of these games, the mouse pointer is context sensitive in that it applies different actions to different objects.[2]

History

Early years

Graphic adventure games were introduced by a company called On-Line Systems, which later changed its name to Sierra On-Line. After the rudimentary *Mystery House* (1980),[3] and the first color adventure game *Wizard and the Princess* (1980), they established themselves with the full adventure *King's Quest* (1984), appearing on various systems, and went on to further success with a variety of strong titles.

A number of games were released on 8-bit home computer formats in the 1980s that advanced on the text adventure style originated with games like *Colossal Cave Adventure* and, in a similar manner to Sierra, added moveable (often directly-controllable) characters to a parser or input-system similar to traditional adventures. Examples of this include Gargoyle Games's *Heavy on the Magick* (1986), which has a text-input system with an animated display screen, the later *Magic Knight* games such as *Spellbound* (1985), which uses a window-menu system for text-adventure style input, the original PC-6001 version of Yūji Horii's murder mystery game *Portopia Serial Murder Case* (1983), and Hideo Kojima's classic *Snatcher* (1988).

Point-and-click adventure

From 1984, a new kind of graphic adventure emerged, following the launch of the Apple Macintosh with its point-and-click interface. The first adventure game to take advantage of the Mac's point-and-click interface was the innovative but relatively unknown *Enchanted Scepters* released the same year, followed in 1985 with the ICOM Simulations game *Deja Vu* that completely banished the text parser for a point-and-click interface. That same year, the NES version of Chunsoft's *Portopia Serial Murder Case* worked around the console's lack of keyboard by taking advantage of its D-pad to replace the text parser of the original 1983 PC-6001 version with a cursor interface for the NES

The Whispered World is a 2009 point-and-click adventure.

version.[4] The following year, Square's *Suishō no Dragon* on the NES took it a step further with its introduction of visual icons and animated scenes.[5] [4]

In 1987, ICOM's well-known second follow-up *Shadowgate* was released, and LucasArts also entered the field with *Maniac Mansion*, a point-and-click adventure that gained a strong following. A prime example of LucasArts' work is the *Monkey Island* series. In 1988, popular adventure game publisher Sierra Online created *Manhunter: New York*. It marked a major shift for Sierra, having used a text parser for their adventure games akin to text adventures. Another famous point-and-click graphic adventure game was Hideo Kojima's *Policenauts* (1994). Point-and-click was used in horror games as well as Human Entertainment's *Clock Tower* series quickly became popular in its first release in 1995. It later branched a sequel and a spin-off.

Graphic adventure games were quick to take advantage of the storage possibilities of the CD-ROM medium and the power of the Macromedia Director multimedia-production software. Games such as *Alice* (1990), *Spaceship Warlock* (1991), *The Journeyman Project* (1993), and *Iron Helix* (1993) incorporated pre-rendered 3D elements and live-action video, as seen to good effect later in *Blade Runner*.

In 1993, *Day of the Tentacle*, a sequel to *Maniac Mansion*, was released. It featured the original game as an Easter egg.

Space Quest IV became the first in the popular series to feature a point-and-click interface. *King's Quest V* was the first for its series. Eventually, the first games in both series would be remade in the point-and-click format with VGA graphics.

Other notable point-and-click adventure games include:

- *Indiana Jones and the Fate of Atlantis* (1992)
- *Freddy Pharkas: Frontier Pharmacist* (1993)
- *Sam & Max Hit the Road* (1993)
- *Gabriel Knight: Sins of the Fathers* (1993)
- *Beneath a Steel Sky* (1994)
- *The Dig* (1995)
- *Torin's Passage* (1995)
- *Broken Sword: The Shadow of the Templars* (1996)
- *Blade Runner* (1997)

First-person adventure

The 1980s also saw the development of first-person-adventure games, similar to point-and-click adventure games, but using a first-person perspective, often featuring limited or no other characters.

By 1993, *Myst* represented a major milestone for graphical adventure games. It featured a first-person viewpoint and reached 6 million sales, making it one of the best selling PC games of all time.[6] [7]

A sequel to *Myst* was later published, known as *Riven*. A satire of *Myst*, known as *Pyst*, was published in response to the success of *Myst*. Another notable first-person-adventure game is *Lighthouse*.

A screen shot from *Myst*, a popular graphic adventure game.

The third installation of *Myst*, entitled *Myst III: Exile*, was released on PC as well as the Microsoft Xbox and Sony PlayStation 2.

Another popular series marketed as a first-person adventure, included the Metroid Prime series from Nintendo, due to the large exploration component of the game and its precedence over combat.[8]

Decline and rebirth

The genre has since seen a relative decline, since the late 1990s, notably in the United States; graphic adventures remain popular in Japan and Europe. Reasons for the decline involve the ability for computer hardware to play more graphically and gameplay advanced action games such as first-person shooters, and the advent of online gaming where players can play against other gamers online. Such online features are irrelevant to adventure gaming. The popularity and sales of these games have made publishers less inclined to fund development teams making graphic adventures for fear of bad sales.

Notable events included Sierra almost entirely shutting down its studio in 1999, and LucasArts ceasing publication after 2000; the *Tex Murphy* franchise was also shelved after 1998. Commercially, *Grim Fandango* (1998) by LucasArts was considered a failure, selling under 100,000 copies in the 5 years after launch – compare with over 500,000 sales of *King's Quest V* (1990) less than a decade earlier – and while LucasArts published one further adventure game (in 2000), it canceled remaining games, dismissed most of the teams involved in 2004,[9] and in 2006 declared that it was exiting the market for the time being and did not plan to make adventure games for another decade.[9] [10]

Recently however independent users have created many smaller graphic adventure games in Adobe Flash, such as the series *Johnny Rocketfingers*, which is one of the most popular point-and-click in Flash on the Internet or the series *The Several Journeys of Reemus* by Jay Ziebarth and the *Submachine* series by Mateusz Skutnik. Many of these challenge the player to interact with objects in an environment. These form very short and basic point-and-click adventure games. A popular sub-genre is known as escape the room games.

The graphic adventure genre has seen a rebirth with the introduction of new video game hardware like the Nintendo DS, and Wii, that allows the gamer to interact with the game similarly to using a computer mouse. As a result, many developers have developed new graphic adventures for these platforms.

Recent examples of graphic adventures include *Zack & Wiki: Quest for Barbaros' Treasure* for the Wii, *Ceville* for the PC, *Broken Sword: The Shadow of the Templars* for the Nintendo DS, as well as games developed by Telltale Games, founded by former LucasArts employees. Their games include *Sam & Max Save the World* and *Sam & Max Beyond Time and Space*, *Strong Bad's Cool Game for Attractive People*, *Wallace & Gromit's Grand Adventures*, the *Monkey Island* revival, *Tales of Monkey Island*, *Back to the Future: The Game*, which came out episodically in five parts, and *Jurassic Park: The Game*, which is set to come out in four parts.

Some recent adventure games have made attempts to revitalize and reinvent the adventure game genre by blending new technologies, interfaces, and gameplay elements into it. RealMyst and several other recent *Myst* games took the *Myst* series into Realtime3D, and *Myst Online: Uru Live* included multiplayer functionality and physics-based puzzles. *Dreamfall*, *Portal*, and many other games have mixed action elements with elements of the adventure genre, blurring genre lines. Some recent adventure games, including *Machinarium* and some of the titles by Telltale Games, have integrated a variety of hint systems into their game design to make the genre more accessible to players.

Japanese development

In Japan this is known as a *Comic Adventure*, in which many of the graphic designers who worked on Comic books (Manga) and animation were able to use their talent on the computer. One such game that makes a great example of this is Metal Slader Glory. Thanks to the efforts of various artists in conjunction with the popularity of Dungeons & Dragons type First Person Shooter games, many revolutionary programs such as Deluxe Paint and Photoshop were actually put to use on actually hand-drawn images rather than typical photographs. These Comic Adventure games is part of the reason why the popularity of point-and-click and FMV games was able to survive.

Parody

The creators of Homestar Runner developed a game known as *Peasant's Quest*.[11] The game is mostly a parody of the first King's Quest game, but also references the second through fourth games in the series. Peasant's Quest also somewhat references Black Cauldron.

See also

* List of graphic adventure games

References

[1] IGN: Escape From Monkey Island (http://ps2.ign.com/objects/016/016196.html)

[2] Rollings, Andrew; Ernest Adams (2006). *Fundamentals of Game Design* (http://wps.prenhall.com/bp_gamedev_1/54/14053/3597646. cw/index.html). Prentice Hall. .

[3] GameSpy.com - Top 10 (http://archive.gamespy.com/top10/march03/genres/index4.shtml)

[4] Gameman (2005-09-06). "" (http://plusd.itmedia.co.jp/games/articles/0509/06/news029.html) (in Japanese). *ITmedia +D Games* (http://plusd.itmedia.co.jp/games/). ITmedia. p. 1. . Retrieved 2007-08-16. (Translation (http://translate. google.co.uk/translate?hl=en&sl=ja&tl=en&u=http://gamez.itmedia.co.jp/games/articles/0509/06/news029.html))

[5] "- SQUARE ENIX" (http://www.square-enix.com/jp/archive/suisho_no_dragon/). Square Enix Japan. . Retrieved 2008-05-26. (Translation (http://translate.google.co.uk/translate?hl=en&sl=ja&tl=en&u=http://www.square-enix.com/jp/archive/ suisho_no_dragon/))

[6] Guilofil, Michael (2001-05-22). "Beyond the Myst" (http://www.spokesmanreview.com/pf.asp?date=052201&id=s966647). The Spokesman-Review. .

[7] Walker, Trey (2002-03-22). "The Sims overtakes Myst" (http://www.gamespot.com/pc/strategy/simslivinlarge/news_2857556.html). CNET Networks. . Retrieved 2008-03-17.

[8] http://www.gamespot.com/gamecube/action/metroid-prime/news.html?sid=6101089

[9] "A Short History of LucasArts" (http://www.next-gen.biz/features/short-history-lucasarts). *Edge*. Future plc. 2006-08-26. . Retrieved 2009-02-02.

[10] "LucasArts at E3" (http://www.g4tv.com/attackoftheshow/videos/11326/LucasArts_at_E3.html). G4tv. 2006. . Retrieved 2008-03-03.

[11] http://www.homestarrunner.com/disk4of12.html

Further reading

* Richard Moss (2011). A truly graphic adventure: the 25-year rise and fall of a beloved genre (http://arstechnica. com/gaming/reviews/2011/01/history-of-graphic-adventures.ars)". *Ars Technica.*

Frictional Games

Type	Privately held
Industry	Gaming industry
Founded	2006
Headquarters	Helsingborg, Sweden
Key people	Thomas Grip and Jens Nilsson
Products	*Penumbra series* *Amnesia: The Dark Descent*
Employees	5
Website	http://www.frictionalgames.com

Frictional Games is an independent video game company located in Helsingborg, Sweden. The developer comprises a small core team and is led by Thomas Grip and Jens Nilsson.[1] Certain key roles such as Music and Narrative Design are performed by external staff like Mikko Tarmia and Tom Jubert, respectively. Linux and Mac OS X ports are handled by Edward Rudd.[2]

Until now, Frictional Games specialized in adventures in the survival horror genre, but the team has stated that it is open for new ideas and game concepts.[3]

All of Frictional's titles employ the in-house game engine HPL. Penumbra itself was originally a tech demo created in 2006 to show off the technology.[4]

Games

Penumbra

- *Penumbra (tech demo)* (non-commercial and downloadable for free) — Windows (2006)
- *Penumbra: Overture* — Windows, Mac OS X, Linux (2007)
- *Penumbra: Black Plague* — Windows, Mac OS X, Linux (2008)
- *Penumbra: Requiem* — Windows, Mac OS X, Linux (2008)

The studio's first commercially released video game was the survival horror game *Penumbra: Overture* in 2007, followed by its sequel *Penumbra: Black Plague* in 2008[5] and finally the expansion *Penumbra: Requiem* later in 2008.[6]

Amnesia: The Dark Descent

- *Amnesia: The Dark Descent* — Windows, Mac OS X, Linux (2010)

In 2010, Frictional Games released their fourth game *Amnesia: The Dark Descent* which introduces version 2 of the HPL Engine.[7]

With the completion of *Amnesia: The Dark Descent*, Frictional Games is currently developing an untitled game, along with version 3 of the HPL Engine.[8]

References

[1] Thomas Grip of Frictional Games Interview (http://questional.com/interview/
     119-thomas-grip-of-frictional-games-head-programmer-master-of-horror/)
[2] Frictional Games, Penumbra: Overture for Linux out now! (http://frictionalgames.com/site/node/42)
[3] Game Central, Interview with Frictional Games (http://game-central.org/2010/editorials/interview-with-frictional-games/)
[4] Frictional Games, Penumbra Tech Demo 2006 (http://frictionalgames.com/site/penumbra)
[5] LinuxGames, Penumbra: Black Plague Final (http://www.linuxgames.com/archives/9995)
[6] LinuxGames, Penumbra: Requiem Released for Linux (http://www.linuxgames.com/archives/11184)
[7] Linux Gaming News, Interview With Frictional Games - Amnesia (http://linuxgamingnews.org/2009/11/25/
     interview-with-frictional-games-amnesia/)
[8] http://frictionalgames.blogspot.com/2010/10/tech-feature-sunlight-with-shadows.html

External links

- Frictional Games official site (http://www.frictionalgames.com/)
- Blog of Frictional Games (http://frictionalgames.blogspot.com/)
- Frictional Games (http://twitter.com/frictionalgames) on Twitter
- Frictional Games (http://www.facebook.com/pages/Frictional-Games/212416275440) on Facebook

Penumbra: Requiem

Penumbra: Requiem	
Developer(s)	Frictional Games
Publisher(s)	Paradox Interactive
Designer(s)	Thomas Grip Jens Nilsson Tom Jubert
Composer(s)	Mikko Tarmia
Series	Penumbra
Engine	HPL
Version	1.1 [1] [2] [3]
Platform(s)	Microsoft Windows, Linux, Mac OS X
Release date(s)	**Microsoft Windows** August 27, 2008 **Linux:** November 17, 2008 **Mac OS X:** November 17, 2008
Genre(s)	Graphic adventure, Survival horror
Mode(s)	Single-player
Media/distribution	DVD, Download

Penumbra: Requiem is an expansion pack to the game *Penumbra: Black Plague* by Frictional Games.[4]

Gameplay

Like the previous games, *Requiem* is an exploration-based adventure game that takes place from a first-person perspective and is the final installment of the main series. Unlike *Black Plague* and *Penumbra: Overture* however, the focus is almost exclusively on puzzle solving. No enemies are encountered meaning the player can only be injured by environmental hazards.

Story

The game starts as the last one ends, with Philip sending the 'kill them all' message. As soon as he finishes, one of the Infected barges in and hits Phillip on the head with something unseen. The player then controls a character in some kind of tomb. Items need to be collected in each chamber in order to move on to the next. In the journey, the player starts to see familiar places from other parts of the facility and begins to receive communications from persons who Philip had encountered previously, such as Dr. Richard Emminis who Philip encountered in the Computer Room of *Black Plague*, a member of the Archaic Elevated Caste called Ellof Carpenter, as well as person who later identifies himself as Philip's former adviser, Red, from the first *Penumbra* game.

As time goes on various strange happenings occur, such as the Computer referring to both Philip and the Player directly by name as well as more bizarre environments and puzzles. The game, and the entire series, has two possible endings. One concludes with Philip joining Red in the incinerator from *Overture*, deeming regular life not worth living. As the rest of *Requiem* seems to have been a figment of Philips mind, this leaves him dead in the room where the game originally began and where *Black Plague* ended. Philip can also choose to leave Red to die on his own, and return to the fishing boat which was originally used to take him to the mine in the first place, or send home safe and sound. This seems to be a fulfilling of Red's statement that it is "better to have a story and end it than never to realize it has begun".

Development

With the announcement of *Penumbra: Black Plague*, the series (originally intended to be a trilogy) was reduced to two episodes due to unidentified problems with the previous publisher, Lexicon Entertainment. After the release of *Black Plague* there continued to be no indication that the developers intended to expand the series other than an April Fools' Day posting about "Penumbra 3 : Back With a Vengeance", a game which would have featured over the top violence and "an action-filled blood soaked ending!"[5]

The developers did however eventually decide that they would release a third installment in the form of an expansion pack in order to tie up loose ends and more fully utilize some of the series characters, as well as to create a more puzzle focused title in order to fully show off the HPL Engine's advanced physics effects.[6] *Penumbra: Requiem* was officially announced on April 16, 2008.[7] During the expansion's development work also began on what would become *Amnesia: The Dark Descent*.[8]

Reception

Penumbra: Requiem was less popular than the previous games in the series, only earning a ranking of 67 from MetaCritic,[9] receiving a rank of only 62 from MobyGames,[10] and a total score of 62.77% from GameRankings.[11] It did however manage to gain the same four star rating as the previous games received from The Linux Game Tome.[12]

References

[1] http://support.frictionalgames.com/entry/85/

[2] http://support.frictionalgames.com/entry/92/

[3] http://support.frictionalgames.com/entry/90/

[4] Interview With Frictional Games – Penumbra/Amnesia (Tgdb.nl) (http://www.tgdb.nl/computer/specials/ 8614-interview-frictional-games.html)

[5] Penumbra 3 - BWaV Announced! (http://www.frictionalgames.com/site/node/62) Frictional Games, April 01, 2008

[6] RPS Interview: Penumbra's Tom Jubert (http://www.rockpapershotgun.com/2008/07/21/rps-interview-penumbras-tom-jubert/) Rock, Paper, Shotgun, July 21, 2008 (Article by John Walker)

[7] 'Penumbra: Requiem' Announced (http://worthplaying.com/article/2008/4/16/news/50470/) Worthplaying, April 16, 2008

[8] Frictional Games On Penumbra And The Future (http://www.rockpapershotgun.com/2009/02/17/ interview-frictional-games-on-penumbra-and-the-future/) Rock, Paper Shotgun, February 17, 2009

[9] Penumbra: Requiem - MetaCritic (http://www.metacritic.com/games/platforms/pc/penumbrarequiem)

[10] Penumbra: Requiem at MobyGames (http://www.mobygames.com/game/penumbra-requiem)

[11] Penumbra: Requiem - GameRankings (http://www.gamerankings.com/pc/945862-penumbra-requiem/index.html)

[12] Penumbra: Requiem - The Linux Game Tome (http://happypenguin.org/show?Penumbra: Requiem)

External links

- Official *Penumbra: Requiem* web-site (http://www.penumbrarequiem.com)
- *Penumbra: Requiem* (http://www.mobygames.com/game/penumbra-requiem) on MobyGames

Microsoft Windows

The latest Windows release, Windows 7, showing the desktop and Start menu	
Company / developer	Microsoft
Programmed in	C, C++ and Assembly language[1]
OS family	Windows 9x, Windows CE and Windows NT
Working state	Publicly released
Source model	Closed source / Shared source
Initial release	November 20, 1985 (as Windows 1.0)
Latest stable release	[[Windows 7 [2]], Windows Server 2008 R2 NT 6.1 (Build 7601: Service Pack 1)] (February 22, 2011) [± [3]]
Latest unstable release	[[Windows 8 [4]] NT 6.2 (Build 8102)] [± [5]]
Marketing target	Personal computing
Available language(s)	Multilingual (listing of available Windows 7 language packs [6])
Update method	Windows Update
Supported platforms	ARM, IA-32, x86-64 and Itanium
Kernel type	Hybrid
Default user interface	Graphical (Windows Shell)
License	Proprietary commercial software
Official website	[windows.microsoft.com windows.microsoft.com]

Microsoft Windows is a series of operating systems produced by Microsoft.

Microsoft introduced an operating environment named *Windows* on November 20, 1985 as an add-on to MS-DOS in response to the growing interest in graphical user interfaces (GUIs).[7] Microsoft Windows came to dominate the world's personal computer market, overtaking Mac OS, which had been introduced in 1984.

The most recent client version of Windows is Windows 7; the most recent server version is Windows Server 2008 R2; the most recent mobile version is Windows Phone 7.

Versions

The term *Windows* collectively describes any or all of several generations of Microsoft operating system products. These products are generally categorized as follows:

The classic Windows logo, used until the release of Windows XP in 2001

Early versions

The history of Windows dates back to September 1981, when Chase Bishop, a computer scientist, designed the first model of an electronic device and project "Interface Manager" was started. It was announced in November 1983 (after the Apple Lisa, but before the Macintosh) under the name "Windows", but Windows 1.0 was not released until November 1985.[8] The shell of Windows 1.0 was a program known as the MS-DOS Executive. Other supplied programs were Calculator, Calendar, Cardfile, Clipboard viewer, Clock, Control Panel, Notepad, Paint, Reversi, Terminal, and Write. Windows 1.0 did not allow overlapping windows. Instead all windows were tiled. Only dialog boxes could appear over other windows.

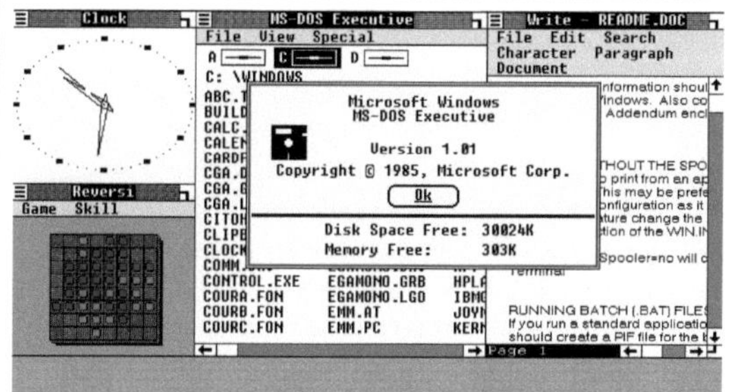

Windows 1.0, the first version, released in 1985

Windows 2.0 was released in October 1987 and featured several improvements to the user interface and memory management.[8] Windows 2.0 allowed application windows to overlap each other and also introduced more sophisticated keyboard shortcuts. It could also make use of expanded memory.

Windows 2.1 was released in two different versions: Windows/386 employed the 386 virtual 8086 mode to multitask several DOS programs, and the paged memory model to emulate expanded memory using available extended memory. Windows/286 (which, despite its name, would run on the 8086) still ran in real mode, but could make use of the high memory area.

The early versions of Windows were often thought of as simply graphical user interfaces, mostly because they ran on top of MS-DOS and used it for file system services.[9] However, even the earliest 16-bit Windows versions already assumed many typical operating system functions; notably, having their own executable file format and providing their own device drivers (timer, graphics, printer, mouse, keyboard and sound) for applications. Unlike MS-DOS, Windows allowed users to execute multiple graphical applications at the same time, through cooperative multitasking. Windows implemented an elaborate, segment-based, software virtual memory scheme, which allowed it to run applications larger than available memory: code segments and resources were swapped in and thrown away when memory became scarce, and data segments moved in memory when a given application had relinquished processor control.

Windows 3.0 and 3.1

Windows 3.0 (1990) and Windows 3.1 (1992) improved the design, mostly because of virtual memory and loadable virtual device drivers (VxDs) that allowed them to share arbitrary devices between multitasked DOS windows. Also, Windows applications could now run in protected mode (when Windows was running in Standard or 386 Enhanced Mode), which gave them access to several megabytes of memory and removed the obligation to participate in the software virtual memory scheme. They still ran inside the same address space, where the segmented memory provided a degree of protection, and multi-tasked cooperatively. For Windows 3.0, Microsoft also rewrote critical operations from C into assembly.

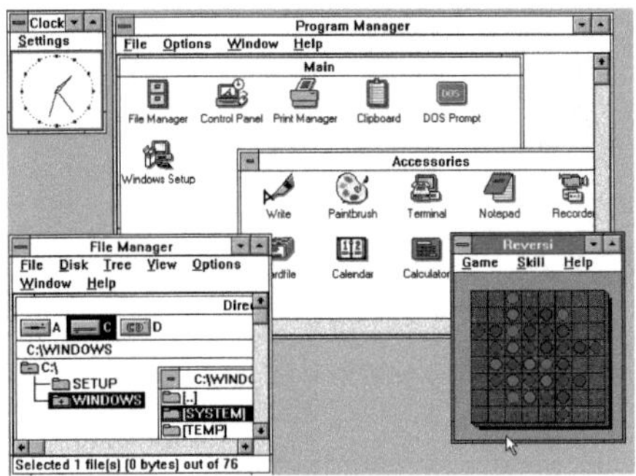

Windows 3.0, released in 1990

Windows 95, 98, and Me

Windows 95 was released in August 1995, featuring a new user interface, support for long file names of up to 255 characters, and the ability to automatically detect and configure installed hardware (plug and play). It could natively run 32-bit applications, and featured several technological improvements that increased its stability over Windows 3.1. There were several OEM Service Releases (OSR) of Windows 95, each of which was roughly equivalent to a service pack.

Microsoft's next release was Windows 98 in June 1998. Microsoft released a second version of Windows 98 in May 1999, named Windows 98 Second Edition (often shortened to Windows 98 SE).

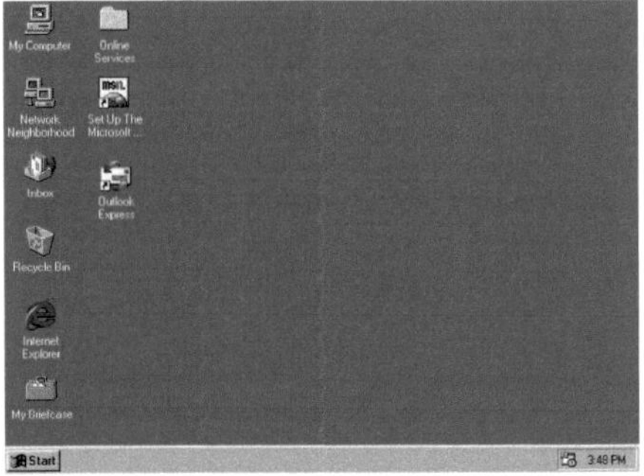

Windows 95, released in August 1995

In February 2000, Windows 2000 (in the NT family) was released, followed by Windows Me in September 2000 (*Me* standing for *Millennium Edition*). Windows Me updated the core from Windows 98, but adopted some aspects of Windows 2000 and removed the "boot in DOS mode" option. It also added a new feature called System Restore, allowing the user to set the computer's settings back to an earlier date.

Windows NT family

The NT family of Windows systems was fashioned and marketed for higher reliability business use. The first release was NT 3.1 (1993), numbered "3.1" to match the consumer Windows version, which was followed by NT 3.5 (1994), NT 3.51 (1995), NT 4.0 (1996), and Windows 2000, which is the last NT-based Windows release that does not include Microsoft Product Activation. Windows NT 4.0 was the first in this line to implement the "Windows 95" user interface (and the first to include Windows 95's built-in 32-bit runtimes).

Microsoft then moved to combine their consumer and business operating systems with Windows XP that was released on October 25, 2001. It came both in home and professional versions (and later niche market versions for tablet PCs and media centers); they also diverged release schedules for server operating systems. Windows Server 2003, released a year and a half after Windows XP, brought Windows Server up to date with Windows XP. After a lengthy development process, Windows Vista was released on November 30, 2006 for volume licensing and January 30, 2007 for consumers. And its server counterpart, Windows Server 2008 was released in early 2008. On July 22, 2009, Windows 7 and Windows Server 2008 R2 were released as RTM (release to manufacturing) while the former was released to the public 3 months later on October 22, 2009.

64-bit operating systems

Windows NT included support for several different platforms before the x86-based personal computer became dominant in the professional world. Versions of NT from 3.1 to 4.0 variously supported PowerPC, DEC Alpha and MIPS R4000, some of which were 64-bit processors, although the operating system treated them as 32-bit processors.

With the introduction of the Intel Itanium architecture (also known as IA-64), Microsoft released new versions of Windows to support it. Itanium versions of Windows XP and Windows Server 2003 were released at the same time as their mainstream x86 (32-bit) counterparts. On April 25, 2005, Microsoft released Windows XP Professional x64 Edition and Windows Server 2003 x64 Editions to support the x86-64 (or *x64* in Microsoft terminology) architecture. Microsoft dropped support for the Itanium version of Windows XP in 2005. Windows Vista was the first end-user version of Windows that Microsoft released simultaneously in x86 and x64 editions. Windows Vista does not support the Itanium architecture. The modern 64-bit Windows family comprises AMD64/Intel64 versions of Windows 7 and Windows Server 2008, in both Itanium and x64 editions. Windows Server 2008 R2 drops the 32-bit version, although Windows 7 does not.

Windows CE

Windows CE (officially known as *Windows Embedded Compact*), is an edition of Windows that runs on minimalistic computers, like satellite navigation systems and some mobile phones. Windows Embedded Compact is based on its own dedicated kernel, dubbed Windows CE kernel. Microsoft licenses Windows CE to OEMs and device makers. The OEMs and device makers can modify and create their own user interfaces and experiences, while Windows CE provides the technical foundation to do so.

Windows CE was used in the Dreamcast along with Sega's own proprietary OS for the console. Windows CE is the core from which Windows Mobile is derived.

The latest current version of Windows CE, Windows Embedded Compact 7, displaying a possible UI for what the media player can look like.

Microsoft's latest mobile OS, Windows Phone, is based on components from both Windows CE 6.0 R3 and the current Windows CE 7.0.

Windows Embedded Compact is not to be confused with Windows XP Embedded or Windows NT 4.0 Embedded, modular editions of Windows based on Windows NT kernel.

Future of Windows

Windows 8, the successor to Windows 7, is currently in development. Microsoft posted a blog entry in Dutch on October 22, 2010 hinting that Windows 8 would be released in roughly 1 year.[10] Also, during the pre-Consumer Electronics Show keynote, Microsoft's CEO announced that Windows 8 will also run on ARM CPUs. This Windows version will also be more suitable for tablets and netbooks, featuring a more touch-friendly interface. Several new features will also be introduced, such as support for USB 3.0 and the ability to run Windows from USB devices (like USB Hard Disks or USB Flash drives) with Windows To Go.

Screenshot of Windows 8 startscreen (Somewhat similar to the Xbox 360 dashboard (as of December 7th, 2011))

Bootable Windows To Go USB flash drive

History

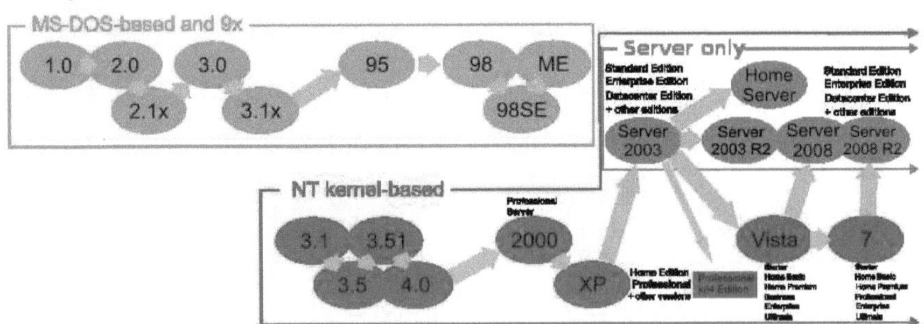

The Windows family tree.

The first version of Microsoft Windows, version 1.0, released in November 1985, lacked a degree of functionality, achieved little popularity and was to compete with Apple's own operating system. Windows 1.0 is not a complete operating system; rather, it extends MS-DOS. Microsoft Windows version 2.0 was released in November 1987 and was slightly more popular than its predecessor. Windows 2.03 (release date January 1988) had changed the OS from tiled windows to overlapping windows. The result of this change led to Apple Computer filing a suit against Microsoft alleging infringement on Apple's copyrights.[11] [12]

Microsoft Windows version 3.0, released in 1990, was the first Microsoft Windows version to achieve broad commercial success, selling 2 million copies in the first six months.[13] [14] It featured improvements to the user interface and to multitasking capabilities. It received a facelift in Windows 3.1, made generally available on March 1, 1992. Windows 3.1 support ended on December 31, 2001.[15]

In July 1993, Microsoft released Windows NT based on a new kernel. Windows NT 3.1 was the first release of Windows NT. NT was considered to be the professional OS and was the first Windows version to utilize preemptive multitasking. Windows NT would later be retooled to also function as a home operating system, with Windows XP.

On August 24, 1995, Microsoft released Windows 95, a new, and major, consumer version that made further changes to the user interface, and also used preemptive multitasking. Windows 95 was designed to replace not only Windows 3.1, but also Windows for Workgroups, and MS-DOS. It was also the first Windows operating system to use Plug and Play capabilities. The changes Windows 95 brought to the desktop were revolutionary, as opposed to evolutionary, such as those in Windows 98 and Windows Me. Mainstream support for Windows 95 ended on December 31, 2000 and extended support for Windows 95 ended on December 31, 2001.[16]

Next in the consumer line was Microsoft Windows 98 released on June 25, 1998. It was followed with the release of Windows 98 Second Edition (Windows 98 SE) in 1999. Mainstream support for Windows 98 ended on June 30, 2002 and extended support for Windows 98 ended on July 11, 2006.[17]

As part of its "professional" line, Microsoft released Windows 2000 in February 2000. During 2004 part of the Source Code for Windows 2000 was leaked onto the Internet. This was bad for Microsoft as the same kernel used in Windows 2000 was used in Windows XP. The consumer version following Windows 98 was Windows Me (Windows Millennium Edition). Released in September 2000, Windows Me implemented a number of new technologies for Microsoft: most notably publicized was "Universal Plug and Play". Windows Me was heavily criticized due to slowness, freezes and hardware problems.

In October 2001, Microsoft released Windows XP, a version built on the Windows NT kernel that also retained the consumer-oriented usability of Windows 95 and its successors. This new version was widely praised in computer magazines.[18] It shipped in two distinct editions, "Home" and "Professional", the former lacking many of the superior security and networking features of the Professional edition. Additionally, the first "Media Center" edition was released in 2002,[19] with an emphasis on support for DVD and TV functionality including program recording and a remote control. Mainstream support for Windows XP ended on April 14, 2009. Extended support will continue until April 8, 2014.[20]

In April 2003, Windows Server 2003 was introduced, replacing the Windows 2000 line of server products with a number of new features and a strong focus on security; this was followed in December 2005 by Windows Server 2003 R2.

On January 30, 2007, Microsoft released Windows Vista. It contains a number of new features, from a redesigned shell and user interface to significant technical changes, with a particular focus on security features. It is available in a number of different editions, and has been subject to some criticism.

On October 22, 2009, Microsoft released Windows 7. Unlike its predecessor, Windows Vista, which introduced a large number of new features, Windows 7 was intended to be a more focused, incremental upgrade to the Windows line, with the goal of being compatible with applications and hardware which Windows Vista was not at the time.[21] Windows 7 has multi-touch support, a redesigned Windows shell with a new taskbar, referred to as the Superbar, a home networking system called HomeGroup,[22] and performance improvements.

Timeline of releases

Usage share

Source	Net Market Share[24]	W3Counter[25]	Global Stats[26]
Date	December 2011	December 2011	December 2011
All versions	92.18%	78.28%	89.97%
Windows 7	36.99%	37.6%	42.65%
Windows XP	46.52%	31.72%	36.44%
Windows Vista	8.44%	8.87%	10.88%
Windows 2000	0.13%	0.09%	—
Windows NT 4.0	0.07%	—	—
Windows 98	0.02%	—	—
Windows Me	0.01%	—	—

Security

Consumer versions of Windows were originally designed for ease-of-use on a single-user PC without a network connection, and did not have security features built in from the outset.[27] However, Windows NT and its successors are designed for security (including on a network) and multi-user PCs, but were not initially designed with Internet security in mind as much, since, when it was first developed in the early 1990s, Internet use was less prevalent.[28]

These design issues combined with programming errors (e.g. buffer overflows) and the popularity of Windows means that it is a frequent target of computer worm and virus writers. In June 2005, Bruce Schneier's *Counterpane Internet Security* reported that it had seen over 1,000 new viruses and worms in the previous six months.[29] In 2005, Kaspersky Lab found around 11,000 malicious programs—viruses, Trojans, back-doors, and exploits written for Windows.[30]

Microsoft releases security patches through its Windows Update service approximately once a month (usually the second Tuesday of the month), although critical updates are made available at shorter intervals when necessary.[31] In versions of Windows after and including Windows 2000 SP3 and Windows XP, updates can be automatically downloaded and installed if the user selects to do so. As a result, Service Pack 2 for Windows XP, as well as Service Pack 1 for Windows Server 2003, were installed by users more quickly than it otherwise might have been.[32]

While the Windows 9x series offered the option of having profiles for multiple users, they had no concept of access privileges, and did not allow concurrent access; and so were not true multi-user operating systems. In addition, they implemented only partial memory protection. They were accordingly widely criticised for lack of security.

The Windows NT series of operating systems, by contrast, are true multi-user, and implement absolute memory protection. However, a lot of the advantages of being a true multi-user operating system were nullified by the fact that, prior to Windows Vista, the first user account created during the setup process was an administrator account, which was also the default for new accounts. Though Windows XP did have limited accounts, the majority of home users did not change to an account type with fewer rights – partially due to the number of programs which unnecessarily required administrator rights – and so most home users ran as administrator all the time.

Windows Vista changes this[33] by introducing a privilege elevation system called User Account Control. When logging in as a standard user, a logon session is created and a token containing only the most basic privileges is assigned. In this way, the new logon session is incapable of making changes that would affect the entire system. When logging in as a user in the Administrators group, two separate tokens are assigned. The first token contains all privileges typically awarded to an administrator, and the second is a restricted token similar to what a standard user would receive. User applications, including the Windows Shell, are then started with the restricted token, resulting in a reduced privilege environment even under an Administrator account. When an application requests higher privileges or "Run as administrator" is clicked, UAC will prompt for confirmation and, if consent is given (including administrator credentials if the account requesting the elevation is not a member of the administrators group), start the process using the unrestricted token.[34]

File permissions

All Windows versions from Windows NT 3 have been based on a file system permission system referred to as AGLP (Accounts, Global, Local, Permissions) AGDLP which in essence where file permissions are applied to the file/folder in the form of a 'local group' which then has other 'global groups' as members. These global groups then hold other groups or users depending on different Windows versions used. This system varies from other vendor products such as Linux and NetWare due to the 'static' allocation of permission being applied directory to the file or folder. However using this process of AGLP/AGDLP/AGUDLP allows a small number of static permissions to be applied and allows for easy changes to the account groups without reapplying the file permissions on the files and folders.

Windows Defender

On January 6, 2005, Microsoft released a Beta version of Microsoft AntiSpyware, based upon the previously released Giant AntiSpyware. On February 14, 2006, Microsoft AntiSpyware became Windows Defender with the release of Beta 2. Windows Defender is a freeware program designed to protect against spyware and other unwanted software. Windows XP and Windows Server 2003 users who have genuine copies of Microsoft Windows can freely download the program from Microsoft's web site, and Windows Defender ships as part of Windows Vista and 7.[35]

Third-party analysis

In an article based on a report by Symantec,[36] internetnews.com has described Microsoft Windows as having the "fewest number of patches and the shortest average patch development time of the five operating systems it monitored in the last six months of 2006."[37]

A study conducted by Kevin Mitnick and marketing communications firm Avantgarde in 2004 found that an unprotected and unpatched Windows XP system with Service Pack 1 lasted only 4 minutes on the Internet before it was compromised, and an unprotected and also unpatched Windows Server 2003 system was compromised after being connected to the internet for 8 hours.[38] This study does not apply to Windows XP systems running the Service Pack 2 update (released in late 2004), which vastly improved the security of Windows XP. The computer that was running Windows XP Service Pack 2 was not compromised. The AOL National Cyber Security Alliance Online Safety Study of October 2004 determined that 80% of Windows users were infected by at least one spyware/adware product. Much documentation is available describing how to increase the security of Microsoft Windows products. Typical suggestions include deploying Microsoft Windows behind a hardware or software firewall, running anti-virus and anti-spyware software, and installing patches as they become available through Windows Update.[39]

Emulation software

Emulation allows the use of some Windows applications without using Microsoft Windows. These include:

- Wine – a free and open source software implementation of the Windows API, allowing one to run many Windows applications on x86-based platforms, including Linux and Mac OS X. Wine developers refer to it as a "compatibility layer";[40] and make use of Windows-style APIs to emulate the Windows environment.
    - CrossOver – A Wine package with licensed fonts. Its developers are regular contributors to Wine, and focus on Wine running officially supported applications.
    - Cedega – TransGaming Technologies' proprietary fork of Wine, designed specifically for running games written for Microsoft Windows under Linux. A version of Cedega known as Cider is used by some video game publishers to allow Windows games to run on Mac OS X. Since Wine was licensed under the LGPL, Cedega has been unable to port the improvements made to Wine to their proprietary codebase. Cedega ceased its service in February 2011.
    - Darwine – A bundling of Wine to the PowerPC Macs running OS X by running Wine on top of QEMU. Intel Macs use the same Wine as other *NIX x86 systems.
- ReactOS – An open-source OS that is intended to run the same software as Windows, originally designed to simulate Windows NT 4.0, now aiming at Windows XP and Vista/7 compatibility. It has been in the development stage since 1996.

See also

- Architecture of the Windows NT operating system line
- Criticism of Microsoft Windows
- Comparison of operating systems
- Comparison of Windows versions
- List of Microsoft Windows components
- List of operating systems
- Wintel

References

[1] "NT Server Training: Architectural Overview. Lesson 2 – Windows NT System Overview." (http://www.microsoft.com/technet/archive/winntas/training/ntarchitectoview/ntarc_2.mspx). *Microsoft TechNet*. Microsoft. . Retrieved December 9, 2010.
[2] http://en.wikipedia.org/wiki/Template%3Alatest_stable_software_release%2Fwindows_nt
[3] http://en.wikipedia.org/wiki/Template%3Alatest_stable_software_release%2Fmicrosoft_windows
[4] http://en.wikipedia.org/wiki/Template%3Alatest_preview_software_release%2Fwindows_nt
[5] http://en.wikipedia.org/wiki/Template%3Alatest_preview_software_release%2Fmicrosoft_windows
[6] http://msdn.microsoft.com/goglobal/ee461121#AvailableLanguagePacks
[7] "The Unusual History of Microsoft Windows" (http://inventors.about.com/od/mstartinventions/a/Windows.htm?rd=1). . Retrieved April 22, 2007.
[8] Petzold
[9] "Windows Evolution" (http://news.soft32.com/windows-evolution_1629.html). Soft32.com News. .
[10] "Microsoft says Windows 8 roughly two years away" (http://news.cnet.com/8301-13860_3-20020544-56.html?tag=mncol;title). *CNET News* (CNET). October 24, 2010. . Retrieved December 9, 2010.
[11] "The Apple vs. Microsoft GUI Lawsuit" (http://lowendmac.com/orchard/06/apple-vs-microsoft.html). 2006. . Retrieved March 12, 2008.
[12] "Apple Computer, Inc. v. MicroSoft Corp., 35 F.3d 1435 (9th Cir. 1994)" (http://home.earthlink.net/~mjohnsen/Technology/Lawsuits/appvsms.html). . Retrieved March 12, 2008.
[13] "Chronology of Personal Computer Software" (http://www.islandnet.com/~kpolsson/compsoft/soft1991.htm). .
[14] "Microsoft Company" (http://www.thocp.net/companies/microsoft/microsoft_company.htm). .
[15] "Windows 3.1 Standard Edition Support Lifecycle" (http://support.microsoft.com/lifecycle/?LN=en-us&p1=3078&x=10&y=11). . Retrieved January 3, 2011.
[16] "Windows 95 Support Lifecycle" (http://support.microsoft.com/lifecycle/?p1=7864). Microsoft. . Retrieved January 3, 2011.

[17] "Windows 98 Standard Edition Support Lifecycle" (http://support.microsoft.com/lifecycle/?p1=6513). Microsoft. . Retrieved January 3, 2011.

[18] David Coursey (August 31, 2001). "Your top Windows XP questions answered! (Part One)" (http://web.archive.org/web/20071219121319/http://review.zdnet.com/4520-6033_16-4206367.html). *ZDNet*. CNET. Archived from the original (http://review.zdnet.com/4520-6033_16-4206367.html) on December 19, 2007. . Retrieved January 3, 2011.

[19] "A Look at Freestyle and Mira" (http://www.winsupersite.com/article/showcase/a-look-at-freestyle-and-mira.aspx). *Paul Thurrott's SuperSite for Windows*. Penton. September 3, 2002. . Retrieved January 3, 2011.

[20] "Windows XP Professional Lifecycle Support" (http://support.microsoft.com/lifecycle/?p1=3223). . Retrieved January 3, 2011.

[21] Mike Nash (October 28, 2008). "Windows 7 Unveiled Today at PDC 2008" (http://windowsteamblog.com/blogs/windows7/archive/2008/10/28/windows-7-unveiled-today-at-pdc-2008.aspx). *Windows Team Blog*. Microsoft. . Retrieved November 11, 2008.

[22] Brandon LeBlanc (October 28, 2008). "How Libraries & HomeGroup Work Together in Windows 7" (http://windowsteamblog.com/blogs/windowsexperience/archive/2008/10/28/how-libraries-amp-homegroup-work-together-in-windows-7.aspx). *Windows Team Blog*. Microsoft. . Retrieved November 11, 2008.

[23] "Windows 98 Second Edition Support Lifecycle" (http://support.microsoft.com/lifecycle/?p1=6898). Microsoft. . Retrieved January 3, 2011.

[24] "Operating System Market Share" (http://marketshare.hitslink.com/operating-system-market-share.aspx?qprid=10&qpcustomd=0&qptimeframe=M&qpsp=155&qpnp=1). *Net Market Share*. Net Applications. December 2011. . Retrieved January 8, 2012.

[25] "Global Web Stats" (http://www.w3counter.com/globalstats.php?year=2011&month=12). *W3Counter*. Awio Web Services. December 2011. . Retrieved January 8, 2012.

[26] "StatCounter Global Stats" (http://gs.statcounter.com/#os-ww-monthly-201112-201112-bar). *Global Stats*. StatCounter. December 2011. . Retrieved January 8, 2012.

[27] Multi-user memory protection was not introduced until Windows NT and XP, and a computer's default user was an administrator until Windows Vista. Source: UACBlog (http://blogs.msdn.com/uac/).

[28] "Telephones and Internet Users by Country, 1990 and 2005" (http://www.infoplease.com/ipa/A0883396.html). Information Please Database. . Retrieved June 9, 2009.

[29] Bruce Schneier (June 15, 2005). "Crypto-Gram Newsletter" (http://www.schneier.com/crypto-gram-0506.html). Counterpane Internet Security, Inc.. . Retrieved April 22, 2007.

[30] Andy Patrizio (April 27, 2006). "Linux Malware On The Rise" (http://www.internetnews.com/dev-news/article.php/3601946). *InternetNews*. QuinStreet. . Retrieved January 3, 2011.

[31] Ryan Naraine (June 8, 2005). "Microsoft's Security Response Center: How Little Patches Are Made" (http://www.eweek.com/c/a/Windows/Microsofts-Security-Response-Center-How-Little-Patches-Are-Made/). *eWeek*. Ziff Davis Enterprise. . Retrieved January 3, 2011.

[32] John Foley (October 20, 2004). "Windows XP SP2 Distribution Surpasses 100 Million" (http://www.informationweek.com/news/security/vulnerabilities/showArticle.jhtml?articleID=50900297). *InformationWeek*. UBM TechWeb. . Retrieved January 3, 2011.

[33] Microsoft describes in detail the steps taken to combat this in a TechNet bulletin. Source: Windows Vista Security and Data Protection Improvements (http://technet.microsoft.com/en-us/windowsvista/aa905073.aspx).

[34] Kenny Kerr (September 29, 2006). "Windows Vista for Developers – Part 4 – User Account Control" (http://weblogs.asp.net/kennykerr/archive/2006/09/29/Windows-Vista-for-Developers-_1320_-Part-4-_1320_-User-Account-Control.aspx). . Retrieved March 15, 2007.

[35] "Windows Vista: Features" (http://www.Microsoft.com/Windowsvista/features/foreveryone/security.mspx). Microsoft. . Retrieved July 20, 2006.

[36] "Symantec Internet Security Threat Report Trends for July – December 2006" (http://eval.symantec.com/mktginfo/enterprise/white_papers/ent-whitepaper_internet_security_threat_report_xi_03_2007.en-us.pdf) (PDF). *Internet Security Threat Report Volume XI*. Symantec. March 2007. . Retrieved January 3, 2011.

[37] Andy Patrizio (March 21, 2007). "Report Says Windows Gets The Fastest Repairs" (http://www.internetnews.com/security/article.php/3667201). *InternetNews*. QuinStreet. . Retrieved January 3, 2011.

[38] "Automated "Bots" Overtake PCs Without Firewalls Within 4 Minutes" (http://www.avantgarde.com/ttln113004.html). *Avantgarde*. Avantgarde. November 30, 2004. . Retrieved January 3, 2011.

[39] Richard Rogers (September 21, 2009). "5 Steps To Securing Your Windows XP Home Computer" (http://www.computer-security-news.com/0969/5-steps-to-securing-your-windows-xp-home-computer). *Computer Security News*. Computer Security News. . Retrieved January 3, 2011.

[40] Wine (http://www.winehq.org/)

External links

- Official website (http://windows.microsoft.com/en-US/windows/home)
- Microsoft Developer Network (http://www.msdn.com/)
- Windows Client Developer Resources (http://msdn.microsoft.com/en-au/windows/default.aspx?WT. mc_id=soc-c-au-loc--2010oct)
- Microsoft Windows History Timeline (http://www.microsoft.com/Windows/WinHistoryIntro.mspx)
- Pearson Education, InformIT (http://www.informit.com/articles/article.aspx?p=1358665&rll=1) – History of Microsoft Windows
- Microsoft Windows 7 for Government (http://www.microsoft.com/industry/government/products/windows7/ default.aspx)

Penumbra: Black Plague

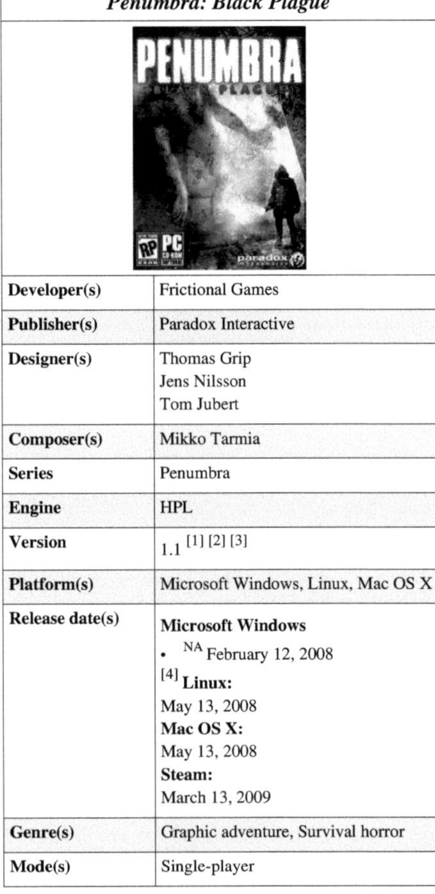

Penumbra: Black Plague	
Developer(s)	Frictional Games
Publisher(s)	Paradox Interactive
Designer(s)	Thomas Grip Jens Nilsson Tom Jubert
Composer(s)	Mikko Tarmia
Series	Penumbra
Engine	HPL
Version	1.1 [1] [2] [3]
Platform(s)	Microsoft Windows, Linux, Mac OS X
Release date(s)	**Microsoft Windows** • NA February 12, 2008 [4] **Linux:** May 13, 2008 **Mac OS X:** May 13, 2008 **Steam:** March 13, 2009
Genre(s)	Graphic adventure, Survival horror
Mode(s)	Single-player

Rating(s)	• ESRB: M • PEGI: 16+
Media/distribution	DVD, Download

Penumbra: Black Plague is the second installment of the *Penumbra* series of episodic computer games developed by Swedish developer Frictional Games. The story continues from the previous episode, *Penumbra: Overture*, showing the protagonist Philip moving away from the abandoned mine setting of the original to explore an underground research base. *Black Plague* was released on February 12, 2008 to generally favourable reviews from critics. Although originally intended to conclude the series, a further expansion called *Penumbra: Requiem* was released later that year.

Gameplay

Black Plague is an exploration-based adventure game that takes place from a first-person perspective.[5] The game's survival horror aspect mostly consists of avoiding various enemies which seek to injure or otherwise harm the protagonist. Compared to the previous game *Overture*, combat has been heavily de-emphasized, with the player no longer able to acquire melee weapons or create makeshift traps to fight enemies with. Instead, the emphasis is on the use of stealth tactics and fleeing to avoid attacks by enemy creatures. Gameplay features a mixture of exploration and solving physical puzzles.

Puzzles vary between traditional inventory puzzles often found in similar games of the adventure genre and primarily physics based puzzles, such as grabbing and stacking boxes in order to build a rudimentary stairway in order to get past a laser tripwire, or placing boards in order to cross an environmental obstruction such as a pit. Unlike in the previous episode, the player must also frequently interact with the bases computer and security systems by acquiring passwords, retrieving biometric data or keycards, and repairing or overriding certain electronic or mechanical devices.

Information is scattered around the base in the form of written notes, recorded messages, saved documents, and various videos and emails that can be found on computers. The protagonist also comes into contact with several survivors which can provide more information and often direct the player to new missions or puzzles. A notebook kept by the protagonist helps keep this information in order and lists the player's current objectives. The protagonist must also overcome distortions to his vision and auditory systems due to his infection, which can cause him to hear or see things that are not there, have distorted sight, or lose some control over his own body. The player must try to overcome these challenges in order to progress through the game.

Plot

The story of *Black Plague* begins as an email sent by Philip to a friend, explaining what has happened to him and begging him to finish the work he could not. The rest of the game then proceeds as a flashback narrated by Philip to his friend in the email, beginning from where the previous game left off.

The game begins with Philip waking up in a locked room, after being knocked out by an unseen being at the end of the first game. Philip manages to escape via a nearby air-vent, and finds himself in the underground research facility of the Archaic Elevated Caste, a secret organization dedicated to discovering and researching ancient knowledge. The base is abandoned and in ruins, with all its personnel either dead or transformed into "the Infected", zombie-like creatures that attack Philip when they notice him. He soon discovers that he has also been infected; however, his reaction to the virus is extremely abnormal; instead of joining the infected hive-mind, he is taken over by the mind of one of the infected, the sarcastic and malevolent Clarence (after the film character) who constantly taunts Philip throughout the course of the game.

Via the base's computer network, Philip is contacted by Dr. Amabel Swanson, an Archaic research scientist who has managed to survive the outbreak by locking herself in her lab. Swanson promises to help cure Philip's infection, if he will make his way to her section of the facility and rescue her.[6] Through dialogue with Swanson, and various scattered documents found throughout the base, Philip learns that the Archaic came to Greenland to look for the "Tuurngait", an ancient entity described in native Inuit mythology as primordial spirits native to the area. Penetrating deep underground, the Archaic found and released the Tuurngait, which manifested as a sentient virus that infected the base's personnel. Philip discovers his father Howard managed to communicate with the Tuurngait, but what he learned drove him to commit suicide after sending Philip a letter ordering him to destroy his research documents.

Philip eventually manages to make his way to Amabel's lab, but Clarence causes him to hallucinate and murder Amabel. Using Amabel's lab notes, Philip manages to rid himself of Clarence by extracting him using a lab machine. However, the machine transfers Clarence into a nearby corpse, which he reanimates and uses to attack Phillip. He is saved by the Tuurngait itself, as several Infected arrive to destroy Clarence, for Clarence now possess an individual body and mind rather than part of "the many" in Tuurngait. The Tuurngait communicates directly with Philip, sending him into his own mind and putting him through a series of spiritual tests designed to test his ability to cooperate, show mercy, and demonstrate self-sacrifice.

Once Philip passes the tests, the Tuurngait reveals all; it is an ancient entity that came to Earth millions of years ago; it once co-existed peacefully alongside the native Inuit, using "Infected" host bodies to pass its ancient knowledge to mankind. However, in time mankind began to grow and expand, and the Tuurngait burrowed underground to separate itself from the human world. When the Archaic came, they disturbed the Tuurngait's ancient slumber and attempted to exploit it, and it fought back against them in self-defense. The Tuurngait explains that mankind is intelligent and compassionate as individuals, but selfish, petty, and destructive as a whole. However, it believes that Philip is different from most of mankind. The Tuurngait puts itself at Philip's mercy, asking him to send a message to someone above ground, for them to destroy all information regarding the Archaic's research facility so that the Tuurngait may rest in peace. This is the same request the Tuurngait made of Philip's father Howard, however Philip thwarted it by coming to investigate instead of following his father's instructions.

Philip seemingly agrees to the Tuurngait's request, and sends an email to a friend on the surface describing his adventure. However, stating that he has more in common with Clarence than with the Tuurngait, Philip gives his friend the coordinates of the mine and tells him to come and destroy the Tuurngait. His last words are: "Kill them. Kill them all."

Development

First intended as a trilogy, the series was reduced to two episodes due to unidentified problems with the previous publisher, Lexicon Entertainment, with the announcement of *Penumbra: Black Plague*. This episode was published by Paradox Interactive. The developers were quite interested in fan feedback during the game's development, which became a driving factor in some of the changes done between *Black Plague* and *Overture*, such as the removal of dogs and other combat related enemies, as well as moving away somewhat from a reliance on written notes.[7] Frictional Games later announced that *Black Plague* was to receive an expansion named *Requiem*, which was released in August 2008.[8]

Reception

Reception	
Aggregate scores	
Aggregator	**Score**
GameRankings	78.90%[9] (PC)
Metacritic	78%[10] (PC)
Review scores	
Publication	**Score**
Adventure Gamers	★ ★ ★ ★ ★ [11]
GameSpot	8.0/10[12]
IGN	7.7/10[13] (PC)
PC Gamer UK	7.4/10[14]
Adrenaline Vault	★ ★ ★ ★ ★ [15]
GamerNode	[16] ★ ★ ★ ★ ★ ★ ★ ★ ★ ★

Black Plague got a slightly better critical reception than its predecessor, holding as of July 2011 a MetaCritic score of 78,[10] a MobyGames rank of 78,[17] and a GameRankings rank of 78.90%.[9] The game also holds a five star rating at The Linux Game Tome.[18]

Black Plague was praised for having a successfully horrific atmosphere and a competently designed and executed plot, with GamerNode raving in one of the games more positive reviews that "the greatest achievement of Black Plague is in its writing. The script never fails to both entertain and enthrall the player, and the game's final, overarching message is profound and well-delivered. I was truly impressed."[16] The removal of the combat system was met with a positive response, with IGN commenting that "without the awkward combat of Overture, Black Plague is a smoother experience where the clumsiness of the physics and control systems are exposed far less frequently."[13] The games use of physics based puzzles was also commented on positively, with PC Gamer deciding that the game's "big sell is the interface, offering the most visceral control over the game-world in any adventure. It's inspired, and when it works, it leaves you begging for other developers to steal it."[14]

Some criticism was directed at the relative shortness of the games campaign and rather abrupt concluding moments, with GameSpot stating that "such brevity and a dissatisfying conclusion might be more forgivable if a third Penumbra was on the way, but this sudden finale is a bit annoying given that this is the end of the line for the series."[12] Adventure Gamers also commented on the game's length, commenting that many "will not relish how short it is", although going on to say that this "isn't necessarily a bad thing, as a certain momentum is maintained throughout, but may give those considering paying in full pause for thought."[11] And while the games graphics and production values were generally thought to look and feel dated, Adrenaline Vault decided that although the visuals in the game can not "compete against the detailed colorful images in a state-of-the art title such as Crysis, they're extremely well-suited for their ominous purpose. The stark, desolate, drab settings allow the game to tell its story convincingly." They also praised the game's sound design, stating that the effects "are simply excellent", the music "is outstanding", and that the "voice acting is also exceptional".[11]

Penumbra: Black Plague was nominated for a Writers' Guild of Great Britain Award in 2008 for Best Video Game Script.[19]

References

[1] http://support.frictionalgames.com/entry/70/

[2] http://support.frictionalgames.com/entry/91/

[3] http://support.frictionalgames.com/entry/89/

[4] "Penumbra to spread to computers again next year" (http://www.adventuregamers.com/newsitem.php?id=1527). Adventuregamers.com. 2007-09-13. . Retrieved 2007-09-20.

[5] Interview With Frictional Games – Penumbra/Amnesia (Tgdb.nl) (http://www.tgdb.nl/computer/specials/8614-interview-frictional-games.html)

[6] Character Postmortem: Amabel Swanson (http://www.tomjubert.com/swanson) Tom Jubert: Writing Portfolio

[7] RPS Interview: Penumbra's Tom Jubert (http://www.rockpapershotgun.com/2008/07/21/rps-interview-penumbras-tom-jubert/) Rock, Paper Shotgun, July 2, 2008 (Article by John Walker)

[8] http://gameplayer.se/news.php?pub_id=10663 News article from Gameplayer.se (swedish)

[9] "*Penumbra: Black Plague* for PC" (http://www.gamerankings.com/pc/943291-penumbra-black-plague/index.html). GameRankings. . Retrieved 2011-07-11.

[10] "*Penumbra: Black Plague* (PC): Reviews" (http://www.metacritic.com/game/pc/penumbra-black-plague). Metacritic. . Retrieved 2011-07-11.

[11] Young, Stuart (2008-02-28). "REVIEW: Penumbra: Black Plague" (http://www.adventuregamers.com/article/id,856). Adventure Gamers. . Retrieved 2011-07-11.

[12] Todd, Brett (2008-02-22). "Penumbra: Black Plague Review" (http://www.gamespot.com/pc/action/penumbrablackplague/review.html). GameSpot. . Retrieved 2011-07-11. (PC)

[13] Onyett, Charles (2008-02-01). "Penumbra: Black Plague Review" (http://pc.ign.com/articles/849/849196p1.html). IGN. . Retrieved 2011-07-11.

[14] Cobbett, Richard (2008-02-28). "Penumbra: Black Plague Review" (http://www.computerandvideogames.com/183630/reviews/penumbra-black-plague-review/). PC Gamer UK. . Retrieved 2011-07-11.

[15] Mandel, Bob (2008-04-11). "Penumbra: Black Plague PC review" (http://www.avault.com/reviews/pc/penumbra-black-plague-pc-review/). Adrenaline Vault. . Retrieved 2011-07-11.

[16] Inzauto, Edward (2008-02-17). "Penumbra: Black Plague Review" (http://gamernode.com/reviews/5968-penumbra-black-plague/index.html). GamerNode. . Retrieved 2011-07-11.

[17] Penumbra: Black Plague at MobyGames (http://www.mobygames.com/game/penumbra-black-plague)

[18] Penumbra: Black Plague - The Linux Game Tome (http://happypenguin.org/show?Penumbra: Black Plague)

[19] http://www.writersguild.org.uk/public/003_WritersGuil/261_WGGBNewsWGG.html Writers' Guild of Great Britain Awards shortlist

External links

- Official Penumbra: Black Plague web-site (http://www.penumbrablackplague.com)
- Penumbra: Black Plague Official Trailer (http://www.paradoxplaza.com/penumbra/)

Mac OS X

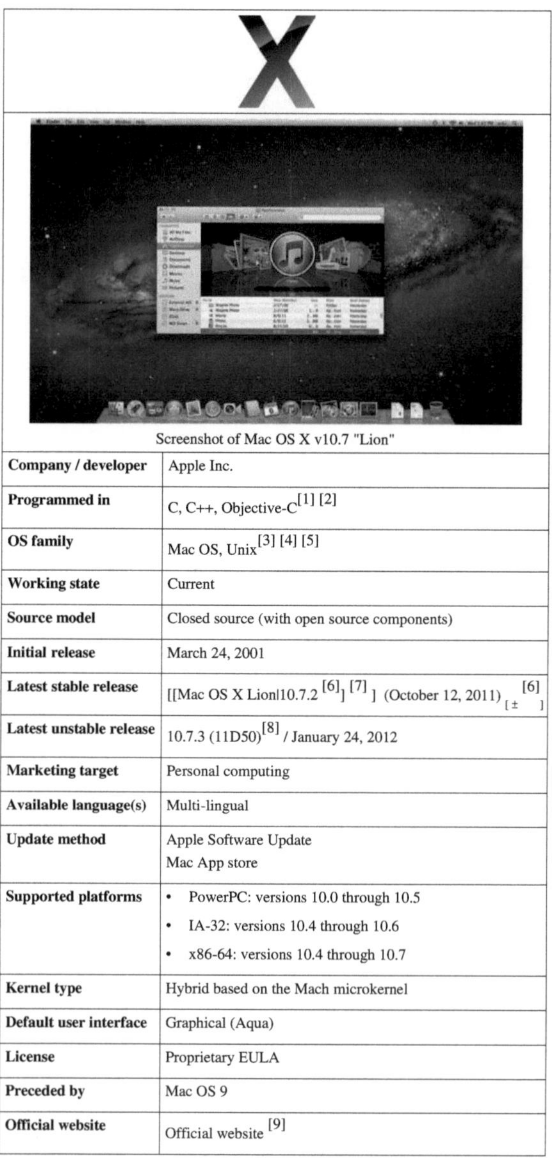

Screenshot of Mac OS X v10.7 "Lion"

Company / developer	Apple Inc.
Programmed in	C, C++, Objective-C[1] [2]
OS family	Mac OS, Unix[3] [4] [5]
Working state	Current
Source model	Closed source (with open source components)
Initial release	March 24, 2001
Latest stable release	[[Mac OS X Lion|10.7.2 [6]] [7]] (October 12, 2011) [± [6]]
Latest unstable release	10.7.3 (11D50)[8] / January 24, 2012
Marketing target	Personal computing
Available language(s)	Multi-lingual
Update method	Apple Software Update Mac App store
Supported platforms	• PowerPC: versions 10.0 through 10.5 • IA-32: versions 10.4 through 10.6 • x86-64: versions 10.4 through 10.7
Kernel type	Hybrid based on the Mach microkernel
Default user interface	Graphical (Aqua)
License	Proprietary EULA
Preceded by	Mac OS 9
Official website	Official website [9]

Mac OS X (/ˈmækˌoʊˌɛsˈtɛn/)[10] is a series of Unix-based operating systems and graphical user interfaces developed, marketed, and sold by Apple Inc. Since 2002, Mac OS X has been included with all new Macintosh computer systems. It is the successor to Mac OS 9, released in 1999, the final release of the "classic" Mac OS, which had been Apple's primary operating system since 1984.

Mac OS X, whose *X* is the Roman numeral for *10* and is a prominent part of its brand identity, is a Unix-based graphical operating system,[11] built on technologies developed at NeXT between the second half of the 1980s and Apple's purchase of the company in late 1996. From its sixth release, Mac OS X v10.5 "Leopard" and onward, every release of Mac OS X gained UNIX 03 certification while running on Intel processors.[3] [4]

The first version released was Mac OS X Server 1.0 in 1999, and a desktop-oriented version, Mac OS X v10.0 "Cheetah" followed on March 24, 2001. Releases of Mac OS X are named after big cats: for example, Mac OS X v10.7 is usually referred to by Apple and users as "Lion". The server edition, Mac OS X Server, is architecturally identical to its desktop counterpart, and includes tools to facilitate management of workgroups of Mac OS X machines, and to provide access to network services. These tools include a mail transfer agent, an LDAP server, a domain name server, and others. It is pre-loaded on Apple's Xserve server hardware, but can be run on almost all of Apple's current selling computer models.[12]

Apple also produces specialized versions of Mac OS X for use on its consumer devices. iOS, which is based on Mac OS X, runs on the iPhone, iPod Touch,[13] iPad, and the second generation Apple TV.[14] An unnamed variant of Mac OS X powered the first generation Apple TV.[15]

History

Mac OS X is based upon the Mach kernel.[16] Certain parts from FreeBSD's and NetBSD's implementation of Unix were incorporated in NeXTSTEP, the core of Mac OS X. NeXTSTEP was the object-oriented operating system developed by Steve Jobs' company NeXT after he left Apple in 1985.[17] While Jobs was away from Apple, Apple tried to create a "next-generation" OS through the Taligent, Copland and Gershwin projects, with little success.[18]

Eventually, NeXT's OS, then called OPENSTEP, was selected to be the basis for Apple's next OS, and Apple purchased NeXT outright.[19] Steve Jobs returned to Apple as interim CEO, and later became CEO, shepherding the transformation of the programmer-friendly OPENSTEP into a system that would be adopted by Apple's primary market of home users and creative professionals. The project was first known as *Rhapsody* and was later renamed to *Mac OS X*.[20]

Mac OS X Server 1.x, was incompatible with software designed for the original Mac OS and had no support for Apple's own IEEE 1394 interface (FireWire). Mac OS X 10.x included more backward compatibility and functionality by including the Carbon API as well as FireWire support. As the operating system evolved, it moved away from the legacy Mac OS to an emphasis on new "digital lifestyle" applications such as the iLife suite, enhanced business applications (iWork), and integrated home entertainment (the Front Row media center).[21] Each version also included modifications to the general interface, such as the brushed metal appearance added in version 10.3, the non-pinstriped titlebar appearance in version 10.4, and in 10.5 the removal of the previous brushed metal styles in favor of the "Unified" gradient window style.[22] [23]

Description

Mac OS X is the tenth major version of Apple's operating system for Macintosh computers. Previous Macintosh operating systems were named using Arabic numerals, e.g. Mac OS 8 and Mac OS 9. The letter *X* in Mac OS X's name refers to the number *10*, a Roman numeral. It is

Box artwork for Mac OS X. Left to right: Cheetah/Puma (1), Jaguar (2), Panther (3), Tiger (4), Leopard (5), and Snow Leopard (6).

therefore correctly pronounced "ten" (/'tɛn/) in this context.[10] [24] However, due to the tenth version being the first to be based on Unix origins, and a reason for the Roman numeral to be used for the number 10 in its honour, a common pronunciation is "X" (/'ɛks/).[25]

Mac OS X's core is a POSIX compliant operating system (OS) built on top of the XNU kernel, with standard Unix facilities available from the command line interface. Apple has released this family of software as a free and open source operating system named Darwin. On top of Darwin, Apple layered a number of components, including the Aqua interface and the Finder, to complete the GUI-based operating system which is Mac OS X.[11]

Mac App Store icon for Lion.

Mac OS X introduced a number of new capabilities to provide a more stable and reliable platform than its predecessor, Mac OS 9. For example, pre-emptive multitasking and memory protection improved the system's ability to run multiple applications simultaneously without them interrupting or corrupting each other.[26] Many aspects of Mac OS X's architecture are derived from OPENSTEP, which was designed to be portable, to ease the transition from one platform to another. For example, NeXTSTEP was ported from the original 68k-based NeXT workstations to x86 and other architectures before NeXT was purchased by Apple,[27] and OPENSTEP was later ported to the PowerPC architecture as part of the Rhapsody project.

The most visible change was the Aqua theme. The use of soft edges, translucent colors, and pinstripes – similar to the hardware design of the first iMacs – brought more texture and color to the user interface when compared to what OS 9 and OS X Server 1.0's "Platinum" appearance had offered. According to John Siracusa, an editor of Ars Technica, the introduction of Aqua and its departure from the then conventional look "hit like a ton of bricks."[28] Bruce Tognazzini (who founded the original Apple Human Interface Group) said that the Aqua interface in Mac OS X v10.0 represented a step backwards in usability compared with the original Mac OS interface.[29] [30] Third-party developers started producing skins for customizable applications and other operating systems which mimicked the Aqua appearance. To some extent, Apple has used the successful transition to this new design as leverage, at various times threatening legal action against people who make or distribute software with an interface the company says is derived from its copyrighted design.[31]

Mac OS X architecture implements a layered design.[32] The layered frameworks aid rapid development of applications by providing existing code for common tasks.

Mac OS X includes its own software development tools, most prominently an integrated development environment called Xcode. Xcode provides interfaces to compilers that support several programming languages including C, C++, Objective-C, and Java. For the Apple–Intel transition, it was modified so that developers could build their applications as a universal binary, which provides compatibility with both the Intel-based and PowerPC-based Macintosh lines.[33]

The Darwin sub-system in Mac OS X is in charge of managing the filesystem, which includes the Unix permissions layer. In 2003 and 2005, two Macworld editors expressed criticism of the permission scheme; Ted Landau called misconfigured permissions "the most common frustration" in Mac OS X,[34] while Rob Griffiths suggested that some users may even have to reset permissions every day, a process which can take up to 15 minutes.[35] More recently, another Macworld editor, Dan Frakes, called the procedure of repairing permissions vastly overused.[36] He argues that Mac OS X typically handles permissions properly without user interference, and resetting permissions should just be tried when problems emerge.[37]

Distribution and languages

As of September 2011, Mac OS X is the second most active general-purpose client operating system in use on the World Wide Web, after Microsoft Windows, with an 8.45% usage share according to statistics compiled by W3Counter.[38] It is the most successful Unix-like desktop operating system on the web, estimated at over 5 times the usage of Linux (which has 1.5%).[38] See also Usage share of operating systems.

There are twenty-two "System Languages" available for the user at the moment of installation (the "system language" is the entire operating system environment). As of Mac OS X Lion, the languages are Arabic, Chinese (Simplified), Chinese (Traditional), Czech, Danish, Dutch, English, Finnish, French, German, Hungarian, Italian, Japanese, Korean, Norwegian, Polish, Portuguese (Brazilian), Portuguese (European), Russian, Spanish, Swedish and Turkish. Input methods for typing in dozens of scripts can be chosen independently of the system language.[39]

Compatibility

Software

The APIs that Mac OS X inherited from OpenStep are not backward compatible with earlier versions of Mac OS. These APIs were created as the result of a 1993 collaboration between NeXT Computer and Sun Microsystems and are now referred to by Apple as Cocoa. This heritage is highly visible for Cocoa developers, since the "NS" prefix is ubiquitous in the framework, standing variously for **Next**step or **NeX**T/**S**un. The official OpenStep API, published in September 1994, was the first to split the API between Foundation and Application Kit and the first to use the "NS" prefix.[27] Apple's Rhapsody project would have required all new development to use these APIs, causing much outcry among existing Mac developers. All Mac software that did not receive a complete rewrite to the new framework would run in the equivalent of the Classic environment. To permit a smooth transition from Mac OS 9 to Mac OS X, the Carbon Application Programming Interface (API) was created. Applications written with Carbon can be executed natively on both systems. Carbon was not included in the first product sold as Mac OS X, Mac OS X Server (now known as Mac OS X Server 1.x).

Mac OS X also used to support the Java Platform as a "preferred software package" — in practice this means that applications written in Java fit as neatly into the operating system as possible while still being cross-platform compatible, and that graphical user interfaces written in Swing look almost exactly like native Cocoa interfaces. Traditionally, Cocoa programs have been mostly written in Objective-C, with Java as an alternative. However, on July 11, 2005, Apple announced that "features added to Cocoa in Mac OS X versions later than 10.4 will not be added to the Cocoa-Java programming interface."[40]

Since Mac OS X is POSIX compliant, many software packages written for the *BSDs, Linux, or other Unix-like systems can be recompiled to run on it. Projects such as Homebrew, Fink, MacPorts and pkgsrc provide pre-compiled or pre-formatted packages. Since version 10.3, Mac OS X has included X11.app, Apple's version of the X Window System graphical interface for Unix applications, as an optional component during installation.[41] Up to and including Mac OS X v10.4 (Tiger), Apple's implementation was based on the X11 Licensed XFree86 4.3 and X11R6.6. All bundled versions of X11 feature a window manager which is similar to the Mac OS X look-and-feel and has fairly good integration with Mac OS X, also using the native Quartz rendering system. Earlier versions of Mac OS X (in which X11 has not been bundled) can also run X11 applications using XDarwin. With the introduction of version 10.5 Apple switched to the X.org variant of X11.[42] Version Mac OS X 10.7 "Lion" use X.org Server version 1.10.x[43]

Hardware

For the early releases of Mac OS X, the standard hardware platform supported was the full line of Macintosh computers (laptop, desktop, or server) based on PowerPC G3, G4, and G5 processors. Later versions discontinued support for some older hardware; for example, Panther does not support "beige" G3s,[44] and Tiger does not support systems that pre-date Apple's introduction of integrated FireWire ports (the ports themselves are not a functional requirement). Mac OS X v10.5 "Leopard", introduced October 2007, has dropped support for all PowerPC G3 processors and for PowerPC G4 processors with clock rates below 867 MHz. Mac OS X v10.6 "Snow Leopard" supports Macs with Intel processors, not PowerPC. Mac OS X 10.7 "Lion" requires a Mac with an Intel Core 2 Duo or newer processor.

Tools such as XPostFacto and patches applied to the installation disc have been developed by third parties to enable installation of newer versions of Mac OS X on systems not officially supported by Apple. This includes a number of pre-G3 Power Macintosh systems that can be made to run up to and including Mac OS X 10.2 Jaguar, all G3-based Macs which can run up to and including Tiger, and sub-867 MHz G4 Macs can run Leopard by removing the restriction from the installation DVD or entering a command in the Mac's Open Firmware interface to tell the Leopard Installer that it has a clock rate of 867 MHz or greater. Except for features requiring specific hardware (e.g. graphics acceleration, DVD writing), the operating system offers the same functionality on all supported hardware.

PowerPC versions of Mac OS X prior to Leopard retain compatibility with older Mac OS applications by providing an emulation environment called Classic, which allows users to run Mac OS 9 as a process within Mac OS X, so that most older applications run as they would under the older operating system. Classic is not supported on Intel-based Macs or in Mac OS X v10.5 "Leopard", but users still requiring Classic applications on Intel Macs can use the SheepShaver emulator to run Mac OS 9 on top of Leopard.

Apple–Intel transition

In April 2002, eWeek announced a rumor that Apple had a version of Mac OS X code-named Marklar, which ran on Intel x86 processors. The idea behind Marklar was to keep Mac OS X running on an alternative platform should Apple become dissatisfied with the progress of the PowerPC platform.[45] These rumors subsided until late in May 2005, when various media outlets, such as the *Wall Street Journal*[46] and CNET,[47] announced that Apple would unveil Marklar in the coming months.

On June 6, 2005, Steve Jobs confirmed these rumors when he announced in his keynote address at the annual Apple Worldwide Developers Conference that Apple would be making the transition from PowerPC to Intel processors over the following two years, and that Mac OS X would support both platforms during the transition. Jobs also confirmed rumors that Apple had versions of Mac OS X running on Intel processors for most of its developmental life. The last time that Apple switched CPU families—from the Motorola 68K CPU to the IBM/Motorola PowerPC—Apple included a Motorola 68K emulator in the new OS that made almost all 68K software work automatically on the new hardware. Apple had supported the 68K emulator for 11 years, but stopped supporting it during the transition to Intel CPUs. Included in the new OS for the Intel-based Macs is Rosetta, a binary translation layer which enables software compiled for PowerPC Mac OS X to run on Intel Mac OS X machines. Apple dropped support for Classic mode on the new Intel Macs. Third party emulation software such as Mini vMac, Basilisk II and SheepShaver provides support for some early versions of Mac OS. A new version of Xcode and the underlying command-line compilers support building universal binaries that will run on either architecture.[48]

PowerPC-only software is supported with Rosetta, though applications may have to be rewritten to run properly on the newer OS X for Intel. Apple initially encouraged developers to produce universal binaries with support for both PowerPC and x86.[49] There is a performance penalty when PowerPC binaries run on Intel Macs through Rosetta. Moreover, some PowerPC software, such as kernel extensions and System Preferences plugins, are not supported on Intel Macs. Some PowerPC applications would not run on Intel OS X at all. Plugins for Safari need to be compiled for the same platform as Safari, so when Safari is running on Intel it requires plug-ins that have been compiled as

Intel-only or universal binaries, so PowerPC-only plug-ins will not work.[50] While Intel Macs are able to run PowerPC, x86, and universal binaries, PowerPC Macs support only universal and PowerPC builds.

Support for the PowerPC platform was dropped after Mac OS X 10.5. Such cross-platform capability already existed in Mac OS X's lineage; OpenStep was ported to many architectures, including x86, and Darwin included support for both PowerPC and x86. Apple stated that Mac OS X would not run on Intel-based personal computers aside from its own, but a hacked version of the OS compatible with conventional x86 hardware was developed by the OSx86 community.

On June 8, 2009, Apple announced at its Worldwide Developers Conference that Snow Leopard (version 10.6) would drop support for PowerPC processors and be Intel-only.[51] However, Rosetta is still available in Snow Leopard; it is not installed by default, but it is available on the installation DVD as an installable add-on and is installed automatically via the Internet when first attempting to run a PowerPC-based application.

In Lion, Rosetta is not available at all.

Features

One of the major differences between the previous versions of Mac OS and OS X was the addition of the Aqua GUI, a graphical user interface with water-like elements. Every window element, text, graphic, or widget is drawn on-screen using anti-aliasing technology.[52] ColorSync, a technology introduced many years before, was improved and built into the core drawing engine, to provide color matching for printing and multimedia professionals.[53] Also, drop shadows were added around windows and isolated text elements to provide a sense of depth. New interface elements were integrated, including sheets (document modal dialog boxes attached to specific windows) and drawers.

Apple has continued to change aspects of the OS X appearance and design, particularly with tweaks to the appearance of windows and the menu bar. One example of a UI behavioral change is that previewed video and audio files no longer have progress bars in column view; instead, they have mouse-over start and stop buttons as of 10.5.

The human interface guidelines published by Apple for Mac OS X are followed by many applications, giving them consistent user interface and keyboard shortcuts.[54] In addition, new services for applications are included, which include spelling and grammar checkers, special characters palette, color picker, font chooser and dictionary; these global features are present in every Cocoa application, adding consistency. The graphics system OpenGL composites windows onto the screen to allow hardware-accelerated drawing. This technology, introduced in version 10.2, is called Quartz Extreme, a component of Quartz. Quartz's internal imaging model correlates well with the Portable Document Format (PDF) imaging model, making it easy to output PDF to multiple devices.[53] As a side result, PDF viewing and creating PDF documents from any application are built-in features.[55]

In version 10.3, Apple added Exposé, a feature which includes three functions to help accessibility between windows and desktop. Its functions are to instantly display all open windows as thumbnails for easy navigation to different tasks, display all open windows as thumbnails from the current application, and hide all windows to access the desktop.[56] Also, FileVault was introduced, which is an optional encryption of the user's files with Advanced Encryption Standard (AES-128).[57]

Features introduced in version 10.4 include Automator, an application designed to create an automatic workflow for different tasks;[58] Dashboard, a full-screen group of small applications called desktop widgets that can be called up and dismissed in one keystroke;[59] and Front Row, a media viewer interface accessed by the Apple Remote.[60] Moreover, the Sync Services were included, which is a system that allows applications to access a centralized extensible database for various elements of user data, including calendar and contact items. The operating system then managed conflicting edits and data consistency.[61]

As of version 10.5, all system icons are scalable up to 512×512 pixels, to accommodate various places where they appear in larger size, including for example the Cover Flow view, a three-dimensional graphical user interface included with iTunes, the Finder, and other Apple products for visually skimming through files and digital media libraries via cover artwork.[62] This version includes Spaces, a virtual desktop implementation which enables the user to have more than one desktop and display them in an Exposé-like interface.[63] Mac OS X v10.5 includes an automatic backup technology called Time Machine, which provides the ability to view and restore previous versions of files and application data;[64] and Screen Sharing was built in for the first time.[65]

Finder is a file browser allowing quick access to all areas of the computer, which has been modified throughout subsequent releases of Mac OS X.[66] [67] Quick Look is part of Mac OS X Leopard's Finder. It allows for dynamic previews of files, including videos and multi-page documents, without opening their parent applications. Spotlight search technology, which is integrated into the Finder since Mac OS X Tiger, allows rapid real-time searches of data files; mail messages; photos; and other information based on item properties (meta data) and/or content.[68] [69] Mac OS X makes use of a Dock, which holds file and folder shortcuts as well as minimized windows. Mac OS X Architecture implements a layered framework.[70] The layered framework aids rapid development of applications by providing existing code for common tasks.[71]

Versions

Mac OS X Version Information

Version	Codename	Date Announced	Release Date	Most Recent Version
Rhapsody Developer Release	Grail1Z4 / Titan1U		August 31, 1997	May 14, 1998
Mac OS X Server 1.0	Hera		March 16, 1999	1.2v3 (October 27, 2000)
Public Beta	Kodiak		September 13, 2000	
10.0	Cheetah		March 24, 2001	10.0.4 (June 22, 2001)
10.1	Puma	July 18, 2001[72]	September 25, 2001	10.1.5 (June 6, 2002)
10.2	Jaguar	May 6, 2002[73]	August 24, 2002	10.2.8 (October 3, 2003)
10.3	Panther	June 23, 2003[74]	October 24, 2003	10.3.9 (April 15, 2005)
10.4	Tiger	May 4, 2004[75]	April 29, 2005	10.4.11 (November 14, 2007)
10.5	Leopard	June 26, 2006[76]	October 26, 2007	10.5.8 (August 5, 2009)
10.6	Snow Leopard	June 9, 2008[77]	August 28, 2009	10.6.8 (June 23, 2011)
10.7	Lion	October 20, 2010[78]	July 20, 2011	10.7.2 (October 12, 2011)

With the exception of Mac OS X Server 1.0 and the original public beta, Mac OS X versions are named after big cats. Prior to its release, version 10.0 was code named "Cheetah" internally at Apple, and version 10.1 was code named internally as "Puma". After the immense buzz surrounding version 10.2, codenamed "Jaguar", Apple's product marketing began openly using the code names to promote the operating system. 10.3 was marketed as "Panther", 10.4 as "Tiger", 10.5 as "Leopard", 10.6 as "Snow Leopard", and the current version 10.7 as "Lion". "Panther", "Tiger" and "Leopard" are registered as trademarks of Apple, but "Cheetah", "Puma" and "Jaguar" have never been registered. Apple has also registered "Lynx" and "Cougar" as trademarks, though these were allowed to lapse.[79] Computer retailer Tiger Direct sued Apple for its use of the name "Tiger". On May 16, 2005 a US federal court in the Southern District of Florida ruled that Apple's use did not infringe on Tiger Direct's trademark.[80]

Public Beta: "Kodiak"

On September 13, 2000 Apple released a $29.95[81] "preview" version of Mac OS X (internally codenamed Kodiak) in order to gain feedback from users.[82]

The "PB" as it was known marked the first public availability of the Aqua interface and Apple made many changes to the UI based on customer feedback. Mac OS X Public Beta expired and ceased to function in Spring 2001.[83]

Version 10.0: "Cheetah"

On March 24, 2001, Apple released Mac OS X v10.0 (internally codenamed Cheetah).[84] The initial version was slow, incomplete, and had very few applications available at the time of its launch, mostly from independent developers. While many critics suggested that the operating system was not ready for mainstream adoption, they recognized the importance of its initial launch as a base on which to improve. Simply releasing Mac OS X was received by the Macintosh community as a great accomplishment, for attempts to completely overhaul the Mac OS had been underway since 1996, and delayed by countless setbacks. Following some bug fixes, kernel panics became much less frequent.

Version 10.1: "Puma"

Later that year on September 25, 2001, Mac OS X v10.1 (internally codenamed Puma) was released.[85] It had better performance and provided missing features, such as DVD playback. Apple released 10.1 as a free upgrade CD for 10.0 users, in addition to the US$129 boxed version for people running Mac OS 9. It was discovered that the upgrade CDs were full install CDs that could be used with Mac OS 9 systems by removing a specific file; Apple later re-released the CDs in an actual stripped-down format that did not facilitate installation on such systems.[86] On January 7, 2002, Apple announced that Mac OS X was to be the default operating system for all Macintosh products by the end of that month.[87]

Version 10.2: "Jaguar"

On August 23, 2002,[88] Apple followed up with Mac OS X v10.2 "Jaguar", the first release to use its code name as part of the branding.[89] It brought great performance enhancements, a sleeker look, and many powerful enhancements (over 150, according to Apple[90]), including Quartz Extreme for compositing graphics directly on an ATI Radeon or Nvidia GeForce2 MX AGP-based video card with at least 16 MB of VRAM, a system-wide repository for contact information in the new Address Book, and an instant messaging client named iChat.[91] The Happy Mac which had appeared during the Mac OS startup sequence for almost 18 years was replaced with a large grey Apple logo with the introduction of Mac OS X v10.2.

Version 10.3: "Panther"

Mac OS X v10.3 "Panther" was released on October 24, 2003. In addition to providing much improved performance, it also incorporated the most extensive update yet to the user interface. Panther included as many or more new features as Jaguar had the year before, including an updated Finder, incorporating a brushed-metal interface, Fast user switching, Exposé (Window manager), FileVault, Safari, iChat AV (which added videoconferencing features to iChat), improved Portable Document Format (PDF) rendering and much greater Microsoft Windows interoperability.[92] Support for some early G3 computers such as "beige" Power Macs and "WallStreet" PowerBooks was discontinued.

Version 10.4: "Tiger"

Mac OS X v10.4 "Tiger" was released on April 29, 2005. Apple stated that Tiger contained more than 150 new features.[93] As with Panther, certain older machines were no longer supported; Tiger requires a Mac with a built-in FireWire port.[44] Among the new features, Tiger introduced Spotlight, Dashboard, Smart Folders, updated Mail program with Smart Mailboxes, QuickTime 7, Safari 2, Automator, VoiceOver, Core Image and Core Video. The initial release of the Apple TV used a modified version of Tiger with a different graphical interface and fewer applications and services. On January 10, 2006, Apple released the first Intel-based Macs along with the 10.4.4 update to Tiger. This operating system functioned identically on the PowerPC-based Macs and the new Intel-based machines, with the exception of the Intel release dropping support for the Classic environment.[94] Only PowerPC Macs can be booted from retail copies of the Tiger client DVD, but there is a Universal DVD of Tiger Server 10.4.7 (8K1079) that can boot both PowerPC and Intel Macs.

Version 10.5: "Leopard"

Mac OS X v10.5 "Leopard" was released on October 26, 2007. It was called by Apple "the largest update of Mac OS X". It brought more than 300 new features.[95] Leopard supports both PowerPC- and Intel x86-based Macintosh computers; support for the G3 processor was dropped and the G4 processor required a minimum clock rate of 867 MHz, and at least 512 MB of RAM to be installed. The single DVD works for all supported Macs (including 64-bit machines). New features include a new look, an updated Finder, Time Machine, Spaces, Boot Camp pre-installed,[96] full support for 64-bit applications (including graphical applications), new features in Mail and iChat, and a number of new security features. Leopard is an Open Brand UNIX 03 registered product on the Intel platform. It was also the first BSD-based OS to receive UNIX 03 certification.[3] [97] Leopard dropped support for the Classic Environment and all Classic applications.[98] It was the final version of Mac OS X to support the PowerPC architecture.

Version 10.6: "Snow Leopard"

Mac OS X v10.6 "Snow Leopard" was released on August 28, 2009. Rather than delivering big changes to the appearance and end user functionality like the previous releases of Mac OS X, Snow Leopard focuses on "under the hood" changes, increasing the performance, efficiency, and stability of the operating system. For most users, the most noticeable changes are: the disk space that the operating system frees up after a clean install compared to Mac OS X 10.5 Leopard, a more responsive Finder rewritten in Cocoa, faster Time Machine backups, more reliable and user friendly disk ejects, a more powerful version of the Preview application, as well as a faster Safari web browser.

The rewrite of Finder in Apple's native Cocoa API allows the Finder to take advantage of the new technologies introduced in Snow Leopard. An update of the web browser, Safari 4, includes a boost in JavaScript and HTML performance, which results in faster web browsing. The majority of this performance boost is enabled by the new SquirrelFish JavaScript interpreter, improving the JavaScript rendering performance of Safari by over 50%.[99] The new Top Sites also displays the most frequently visited and/or bookmarked sites in a panorama view, allowing the user to easily access their favorite sites along with a new Cover Flow view for the user's browsing history. Safari 4 is now also more crash resistant, being able to isolate plug-ins which are the main cause of web browser crashes.[100]

Mac OS X v10.6 also features Microsoft Exchange Server support for Mail, iCal, and Address Book, new 64-bit technology capable of supporting greater amounts of RAM, an all new QuickTime X with a refreshed user interface and more functionality that used to be only available to QuickTime Pro owners.

Back-end platform changes include improved support for multi-core processors through Grand Central Dispatch which attempts to ease the development of applications with multi-core support, and thus improve their CPU utilization. It used to be that developers needed to code their programs in such a way that their software would explicitly take advantage of the multiple cores, which could easily become a tedious and troublesome task, especially in complex software. It also includes advanced GPU performance with OpenCL (a cross platform open standard for

GPGPU distinct from CUDA, Dx11 Compute Shader or STREAM) by providing support to offload work normally only destined for a CPU to the graphic card's GPU. This can be especially useful in tasks that can be heavily parallelized.

Snow Leopard only supports machines with Intel CPUs, requires at least 1 GB of RAM, and drops default support for applications built for the PowerPC architecture (Rosetta can be installed as an additional component to retain support for PowerPC-only applications).[101]

A Snow Leopard update introduced support for the Mac App Store, Apple's digital distribution platform for MacOS X applications.[102]

Version 10.7: "Lion"

Mac OS X v10.7 "Lion" was released on July 20, 2011. It brought developments made in Apple's iOS, such as an easily-navigable display of installed applications (Launchpad) and (a greater use of) multi-touch gestures, to the Mac. This release removed Rosetta, making it incapable of running PowerPC applications.

Changes made to the GUI (Graphical User Interface) include the Launchpad (similar to the home screen of iOS devices), auto-hiding scrollbars that only appear when they are being used, and Mission Control, which unifies Exposé, Spaces, Dashboard, and full-screen applications within a single interface.[103] Apple also made changes to applications: they resume in the same state as they were before they were closed (similar to iOS). Documents auto-save by default.

See also

* A/UX
* Comparison of BSD operating systems
* Comparison of operating systems
* List of Mac OS X technologies
* List of Macintosh software
* List of operating systems
* Market share of operating systems
* Dock (Mac OS X)

References

[1] "Apple Developer: Cocoa Overview" (http://developer.apple.com/Cocoa/overview.html). Apple Inc. . Retrieved April 9, 2010.
[2] "Apple Developer: Mac OS X Technology Overview" (http://developer.apple.com/mac/library/documentation/MacOSX/Conceptual/
     OSX_Technology_Overview/OSX_Technology_Overview.pdf). Apple Inc. . Retrieved April 9, 2010.
[3] "Mac OS X 10.5 on Intel-based Macintosh computers" (http://www.opengroup.org/openbrand/register/brand3555.htm). The Open
     Group. . Retrieved November 22, 2009.
[4] "Mac OS X 10.6 on Intel-based Macintosh computers" (http://www.opengroup.org/openbrand/register/brand3581.htm). The Open
     Group. . Retrieved April 7, 2010.
[5] "Apple page on UNIX" (http://www.apple.com/server/macosx/technology/unix.html). Apple Inc. . Retrieved November 5, 2008.
[6] http://en.wikipedia.org/wiki/Template%3Alatest_stable_software_release%2Fmac_os_x
[7] http://www.apple.com/macosx/
[8] "Apple Seeds OS X 10.7.3 Build 11D50 to Developers" (http://9to5mac.com/2012/01/24/
     apple-seeds-os-x-lion-10-7-3-build-11d50-to-developers/). . Retrieved January 24, 2012.
[9] http://www.apple.com/macosx/
[10] "What is an operating system (OS)?" (http://support.apple.com/kb/TA22541). Apple Inc. July 15, 2004. . Retrieved December 20, 2006.
     "The current version of Mac OS is Mac OS X (pronounced "Mac O-S ten")."
[11] "Mac OS X for UNIX Users" (http://images.apple.com/macosx/pdf/L355785A_UNIX_TB.pdf) (PDF). Apple Inc. March 19. .
     Retrieved September 14, 2009.
[12] "Apple – Mac OS X Server Snow Leopard – Technical Specifications" (http://www.apple.com/server/macosx/specs.html). . Retrieved
     November 22, 2009.

[13] Haslam, Karen (January 2007). "Macworld Expo: Optimised OS X sits on 'versatile' flash" (http://www.macworld.co.uk/ipod-itunes/
news/index.cfm?newsid=16927). Macworld. . Retrieved January 13, 2007.

[14] Foresman, Chris (September 2010). "Apple TV definitely running iOS, could be jailbreak target" (http://arstechnica.com/apple/news/
2010/09/apple-tv-definitely-running-ios-could-be-jailbreak-target.ars). Ars Technica. . Retrieved Nov 16, 2010.

[15] Mossberg, Walter S. (March 21, 2007). "From PC to TV − via Apple" (http://solution.allthingsd.com/20070321/pc-tv-via-apple/). *All
Things Digital*. . Retrieved May 18, 2008.

[16] "Leopard OS Foundations Overview" (http://developer.apple.com/leopard/overview/osfoundations.html). Apple Inc. October 26, 2007.
. Retrieved December 15, 2008.

[17] Singh, Amit. "Architecture of Mac OS X" (http://www.kernelthread.com/mac/osx/arch.html). *What is Mac OS X?*. . Retrieved April 7,
2006.

[18] "Apple Facts" (http://www.theapplemuseum.com/index.php?id=44). The Apple Museum. . Retrieved December 15, 2008. "a joint
venture with IBM, called Taligent, but was discontinued soon thereafter"

[19] Markoff, John (December 23, 1996). "Why Apple Sees Next as a Match Made in Heaven" (http://query.nytimes.com/gst/fullpage.
html?res=9F06E1D71331F930A15751C1A960958260). *The New York Times*: p. D1. .

[20] Anguish, Scott (July 9, 1998). "Apple Renames Rhapsody, now Mac OS X Server" (http://www.stepwise.com/Articles/Business/
RhapsodyRenamed.html). . Retrieved December 20, 2006.

[21] Spolsky, Joel (June 13, 2004). "How Microsoft Lost the API War" (http://www.joelonsoftware.com/articles/APIWar.html). . Retrieved
April 15, 2009. "The developers of the Macintosh OS at Apple have always been in this camp [i.e. not trying to be backwards compatible no
matter what]. It's why so few applications from the early days of the Macintosh still work..."

[22] W., Jeff (May 27, 2008). "Mac OS X (10.5) − User Interface Changes" (http://helpdesk.wisc.edu/page.php?id=6609). University of
Wisconsin. . Retrieved April 15, 2009.

[23] Rizzo, John (November 12, 2003). "Mac OS X 10.3 Panther" (http://www.builderau.com.au/news/soa/Mac-OS-X-10-3-Panther/
0,339028227,320280883,00.htm). . Retrieved April 15, 2009. "Once you reboot, you'll notice that Apple has abandoned the light and airy
Aqua interface for the darker, heavier brushed-metal look of iTunes."

[24] Siracusa, John (March 24, 2006). "Five years of Mac OS X" (http://arstechnica.com/apple/reviews/2006/03/osx-fiveyears.ars). Ars
Technica. . Retrieved April 15, 2009. "Even Steve Jobs still says "ecks" instead of "ten" sometimes."

[25] Kelly, Spencer (February 26, 2011 time: 00:12:45). "BBC Click programme" (http://www.bbc.co.uk/iplayer/episode/b00z8dnj/
Click_26_02_2011/). BBC. . Retrieved March 20, 2011. "Now we have dealt with this a number of times over the years. Of course X (/ˈɛks/)
does mean 10, but anyone who used to poke around on Unix systems will know that in those days anything Unix had an X (ˈɛks) in it, and OS
Ten is written OS X (ˈɛks) in honour of the fact that it is based on Unix, unlike its predecessors. So, hey, you can say it any way you want;
me, I'm showing my age and sticking with X (ˈɛks)."

[26] Raymond, Eric Steven. "The Elements of Operating-System Style" (http://www.faqs.org/docs/artu/ch03s01.html#id2892085). .
Retrieved November 5, 2008.

[27] "Cocoa Fundamentals Guide: A Bit of History" (http://developer.apple.com/documentation/Cocoa/Conceptual/CocoaFundamentals/
WhatIsCocoa/chapter_2_section_6.html#//apple_ref/doc/uid/TP40002974-CH3-SW12). *ADC Reference Library*. Apple Developer
Connection. . Retrieved December 15, 2008.

[28] Siracusa, John (October 28, 2007). "Mac OS X 10.5 Leopard: the Ars Technica review" (http://arstechnica.com/reviews/os/
mac-os-x-10-5.ars/3). Ars Technica. . Retrieved December 16, 2008.

[29] Tognazzini, Bruce (February 2000). "OS X: A First Look" (http://www.asktog.com/columns/034OSX-FirstLook.html). . Retrieved
November 5, 2008.

[30] Thomas, Matthew Paul (February 16, 2004). "My first 48 hours enduring Mac OS X" (http://mpt.net.nz/archive/2004/02/16/os-x). .
Retrieved November 5, 2008.

[31] "Apple lowers boom on Aqua 'skins'" (http://web.archive.org/web/20011031104835/http://www.zdnet.com/zdnn/stories/
newsbursts/0,7407,2681914,00.html?chkpt=p1bn). ZDNet (mirrored from web.archive.org). February 2, 2001. Archived from the original
(http://www.zdnet.com/zdnn/stories/newsbursts/0,7407,2681914,00.html?chkpt=p1bn) on October 31, 2001. . Retrieved May 22, 2006.

[32] "Apple.com" (http://developer.apple.com/mac/library/documentation/MacOSX/Conceptual/OSX_Technology_Overview/
MacOSXOverview/MacOSXOverview.html#//apple_ref/doc/uid/TP40001067-CH205-BCICAIFJ). Developer.apple.com. . Retrieved
June 21, 2011.

[33] "Adopting Universal Binaries on Mac OS X" (http://developer.apple.com/macosx/adoptinguniversalbinaries.html). Apple Inc. February
22, 2007. . Retrieved December 15, 2008.

[34] Landau, Ted (February 2003). "Exterminate OS X Troubles" (http://www.accessmylibrary.com/coms2/summary_0286-23097965_ITM).
Macworld. . Retrieved February 8, 2009.

[35] Griffiths, Rob (February 2005). "Prevent Mac Disasters" (http://www.macworld.com/article/42286/2005/01/preventmacdisasters.
html). *Macworld*. . Retrieved February 8, 2009.

[36] Frakes, Dan (August 2006). "Repairing permissions: what you need to know" (http://www.macworld.com/article/52220/2006/08/
repairpermissions.html). *Macworld*. . Retrieved February 8, 2009.

[37] Frakes, Dan (June 2008). "Five Mac maintenance myths" (http://www.macworld.com/article/133684/2008/06/maintenance_intro.
html). *Macworld*. . Retrieved February 8, 2009.

[38] "Global Web Stats" (http://w3counter.com/globalstats.php). *Operating System Market Share*. W3Counter. September 2011. . Retrieved October 28, 2011.

[39] "System – New system languages." (http://www.apple.com/macosx/whats-new/features.html#system). Apple Inc.. . Retrieved June 6, 2011.

[40] "Introduction to Cocoa-Java Integration Guide" (http://developer.apple.com/documentation/Cocoa/Conceptual/LanguageIntegration/index.html). *ADC Reference Library*. Apple Developer Connection. . Retrieved April 8, 2006.

[41] "X11 for Mac OS X 1.0" (http://support.apple.com/downloads/X11_for_Mac_OS_X_1_0). Apple Inc. October 28, 2003. . Retrieved December 15, 2008.

[42] Ben Byer (October 27, 2007). "Re: X11 in Leopard: xterm on start-up" (http://lists.apple.com/archives/x11-users/2007/Oct/msg00065.html). *Apple's x11-users mailing list*. . Retrieved January 18, 2008.

[43] Michael Larabel (May 28, 2011). "X.Org Server 1.10.2 Brings A Bunch Of Bug-Fixes" (http://www.phoronix.com/scan.php?page=news_item&px=OTQ5OA). phoronix. . Retrieved May 29, 2011.

[44] "Mac OS X: System Requirements" (http://docs.info.apple.com/article.html?artnum=106163). Apple Inc. April 28, 2005. . Retrieved December 20, 2006.

[45] Rothenbourg, Matthew; dePlume, Nick (August 30, 2002). "Apple Keeps x86 Torch Lit with 'Marklar'" (http://www.eweek.com/c/a/Past-News/Apple-Keeps-x86-Torch-Lit-with-Marklar). eWeek.com. . Retrieved October 3, 2005.

[46] Clark, Don; Wingfield, Nick (May 23, 2005). "Apple Explores Use Of Chips From Intel For Macintosh Line" (http://online.wsj.com/article/SB111680203134440188.html). *Wall Street Journal*. . Retrieved February 8, 2009.

[47] Kanellos, Michael (May 23, 2005). "Apple to Intel: Some advantage, lots of risk" (http://www.news.com/2100-1006_3-5716696.html). CNet. . Retrieved April 28, 2006.

[48] "Apple to Use Intel Microprocessors Beginning in 2006" (http://www.apple.com/pr/library/2005/jun/06intel.html). Apple Inc. June 6, 2005. . Retrieved April 8, 2006.

[49] "Adopting Universal Binaries" (http://developer.apple.com/macosx/adoptinguniversalbinaries.html). Apple Inc. January 2006. . Retrieved December 20, 2006.

[50] Landau, Ted (May 2006). "OS X First Aid" (http://www.macworld.com/article/50339/2006/04/firstaidintel.html). *Macworld*. . Retrieved February 8, 2009.

[51] Stevens, Tim (June 10, 2009). "Snow Leopard officially puts PowerPC Macs on endangered species list" (http://www.engadget.com/2009/06/10/snow-leopard-officially-puts-powerpc-macs-on-endangered-species/). *Engadget*. . Retrieved June 15, 2009.

[52] "The Aqua Interface" (http://developer.apple.com/documentation/UserExperience/Conceptual/AppleHIGuidelines/XHIGPartIII/chapter_11_section_1.html). *Apple Human Interface Guidelines*. Apple Inc. June 9, 2008. . Retrieved December 16, 2008.

[53] Davidson, James Duncan (2002). *Learning Cocoa With Objective-C*. O'Reilly. p. 6. ISBN 0596003013.

[54] O'Malley, Kevin (2003). *Programming Mac OS X: A Guide for Unix Developers*. Manning. p. 7. ISBN 1930110855.

[55] "what-is-macosx" (http://www.apple.com/macosx/what-is-macosx/). Apple Inc. . Retrieved March 2, 2011.

[56] "Mac 101: Exposé" (http://support.apple.com/kb/HT2503). Apple Inc. October 31, 2008. . Retrieved December 16, 2008.

[57] "About FileVault" (http://docs.info.apple.com/article.html?path=Mac/10.5/en/8727.html). *Mac OS X 10.5 Help*. Apple Inc. . Retrieved December 16, 2008.

[58] "Mac 101: Automator" (http://support.apple.com/kb/HT2488). Apple Inc. November 6, 2008. . Retrieved December 16, 2008.

[59] "Mac 101: Dashboard" (http://support.apple.com/kb/HT2492). Apple Inc. November 11, 2008. . Retrieved December 16, 2008.

[60] "Front Row" (http://www.apple.com/macosx/features/300.html#frontrow). Apple Inc. . Retrieved December 16, 2008.

[61] "Why Use Sync Services?" (http://developer.apple.com/documentation/Cocoa/Conceptual/SyncServices/Articles/WhySyncServices.html). Apple Inc. October 31, 2007. . Retrieved December 16, 2008.

[62] "Creating Icons" (http://developer.apple.com/documentation/UserExperience/Conceptual/AppleHIGuidelines/XHIGIcons/chapter_15_section_8.html). *Apple Human Interface Guidelines*. Apple Inc. June 9, 2008. . Retrieved December 16, 2008.

[63] "Spaces. Room for everything." (http://www.apple.com/macosx/features/spaces.html). Apple Inc. . Retrieved December 16, 2008.

[64] "Time Machine. A giant leap backward." (http://www.apple.com/macosx/features/timemachine.html). Apple Inc. . Retrieved December 16, 2008.

[65] "Finder" (http://www.apple.com/macosx/features/300.html#finder). Apple Inc. . Retrieved December 16, 2008.

[66] Holwerda, Thom (December 6, 2007). "Review: Mac OS X 10.5 Leopard" (http://www.osnews.com/story/18992/Review_Mac_OS_X_10_5_Leopard/page2/). OS News. . Retrieved April 15, 2009. "The next area where Apple claims to have made major improvements is the Finder."

[67] Siracusa, John (January 26, 2006). "Finding Leopard" (http://arstechnica.com/staff/fatbits/2006/01/2673.ars). Ars Technica. . Retrieved April 15, 2009. "Unsurprisingly, each new Mac OS X release has been the vehicle for a parade of Finder fantasies."

[68] Siracusa, John (April 28, 2005). "Mac OS X 10.4 Tiger" (http://arstechnica.com/apple/reviews/2005/04/macosx-10-4.ars/9). Ars Technica. . Retrieved April 15, 2009.

[69] "Mac 101: Spotlight" (http://support.apple.com/kb/HT2531). Apple Inc. November 6, 2008. . Retrieved April 15, 2009.

[70] "A Layered Approach" (http://developer.apple.com/documentation/MacOSX/Conceptual/OSX_Technology_Overview/MacOSXOverview/chapter_2_section_2.html). Apple Inc. October 15, 2008. . Retrieved February 8, 2009.

[71] Zepko, Tom (November 6, 2003). "Why Cocoa?" (http://homepage.mac.com/tom_zepko/cocoa/why-cocoa.html). . Retrieved April 15, 2009.

[72]   "Apple Previews Next Version of Mac OS X" (http://www.apple.com/pr/library/2001/jul/18macosx.html). Apple Inc.. July 18, 2001. . Retrieved March 11, 2010.

[73]   "Apple Previews "Jaguar", the Next Major Release of Mac OS X" (http://www.apple.com/pr/library/2002/may/06jaguar.html). Apple Inc.. May 6, 2002. . Retrieved March 11, 2010.

[74]   "Apple Previews Mac OS X "Panther"" (http://www.apple.com/pr/library/2003/jun/23panther.html). Apple Inc.. June 23, 2003. . Retrieved March 11, 2010.

[75]   "Steve Jobs to Kick Off Apple's Worldwide Developers Conference 2004 with Preview of Mac OS X "Tiger"" (http://www.apple.com/pr/library/2004/may/04wwdc.html). Apple Inc.. . Retrieved March 11, 2010.

[76]   "Apple Executives to Preview Mac OS X "Leopard" at WWDC 2006 Keynote" (http://www.apple.com/pr/library/2006/jun/26wwdc.html). Apple Inc.. . Retrieved March 11, 2010.

[77]   "Apple Previews Mac OS X Snow Leopard to Developers" (http://www.apple.com/pr/library/2008/06/09snowleopard.html). Apple Inc.. June 9, 2008. . Retrieved March 11, 2010.

[78]   "Apple Gives Sneak Peek of Mac OS X Lion" (http://www.apple.com/pr/library/2010/10/20lion.html). Apple Inc.. October 20, 2010. . Retrieved October 20, 2010.

[79]   Trademark #78257226 for Panther, #78269988 for Tiger, #78270003 for Leopard, #78271630 for Cougar and #78271639 for Lynx, all registered in 2004 by Apple Computer, Inc. "United States Patent and Trademark Office" (http://www.uspto.gov/index.html). . Retrieved December 20, 2006.

[80]   Kasper, Jade. "Court sides with Apple over "Tiger" trademark dispute" (http://www.appleinsider.com/articles/05/05/13/court_sides_with_apple_over_tiger_trademark_dispute.html). AppleInsider. . Retrieved April 25, 2006.

[81]   John Siracusa. "Mac OS X Beta – Page 1 – (10/2000)" (http://arstechnica.com/reviews/4q00/macosx-pb1/macos-x-beta-1.html). Ars Technica. . Retrieved March 11, 2010.

[82]   "Makefile" (http://www.opensource.apple.com/darwinsource/DevToolsJun2005/gas-590/Makefile). Apple Inc. June 2005. . Retrieved December 15, 2008. "RC Release is Kodiak (Public Beta)"

[83]   "Mac OS X Public Beta Expires Today | News" (http://www.macobserver.com/tmo/article/Mac_OS_X_Public_Beta_Expires_Today/). The Mac Observer. . Retrieved March 11, 2010.

[84]   Although the version is now called Cheetah by users, rare evidences can be found to prove that it was called so internally. For instance, a Q&A was created in 2005 which mentions it "Technical Q&A" (http://developer.apple.com/qa/qa2004/qa1378.html). Apple Inc. October 4, 2005. . Retrieved December 20, 2006.

[85]   The name Puma can be found here "Cross-Development" (http://developer.apple.com/documentation/DeveloperTools/Conceptual/cross_development/Using/chapter_3_section_4.html). Apple Inc. November 11, 2006. . Retrieved December 20, 2006.

[86]   "Apple Cease-And-Desists Stupidity Leak" (http://apple.slashdot.org/article.pl?sid=01/11/29/1522209). Slashdot. 2001. . Retrieved November 5, 2008.

[87]   "Apple Makes Mac OS X the Default Operating System on All Macs" (http://www.apple.com/pr/library/2002/jan/07macosx.html). Apple Inc. January 2002. . Retrieved December 3, 2006.

[88]   "Jaguar "Unleashed" at 10:20 pm Tonight" (http://www.apple.com/pr/library/2002/aug/23jaguar.html). Apple Inc. August 23, 2002. . Retrieved December 15, 2008.

[89]   The headline of the press release mention "Jaguar", while the codename was not mentioned for earlier versions. See Apple.com (http://www.apple.com/pr/library/2002/may/06jaguar.html), "Jaguar" press release, compared to Mac OS X v10.0 press release (http://www.apple.com/pr/library/2001/jan/09macosx.html) and Mac OS X v10.1 press release (http://www.apple.com/pr/library/2001/sep/25osx_available.html)

[90]   "Wayback Machine's Cache of the OS X 10.2 Product Information Page" (http://web.archive.org/web/20020829042532/www.apple.com/macosx/). Apple Inc. August 29, 2002. Archived from the original (http://www.apple.com/macosx/) on August 29, 2002. . Retrieved June 12, 2008.

[91]   "Apple Previews "Jaguar," the Next Major Release of Mac OS X" (http://www.apple.com/pr/library/2002/may/06jaguar.html). Apple Inc. May 6, 2002. . Retrieved December 20, 2006.

[92]   "Apple Announces Mac OS X "Panther"" (http://www.apple.com/pr/library/2003/oct/08panther.html). Apple Inc. October 8, 2003. . Retrieved January 11, 2007.

[93]   "Apple Unleashes "Tiger Friday at 6:00 pm" (http://www.apple.com/pr/library/2005/apr/28tiger.html). Apple Inc. April 28, 2005. . Retrieved January 11, 2007.

[94]   "Apple unveils Intel iMacs" (http://www.appleinsider.com/articles/06/01/10/apple_unveils_intel_imacs.html). AppleInsider. January 2006. . Retrieved December 15, 2008.

[95]   "Apple – Mac OS X Leopard – Features – 300+ New Features" (http://www.apple.com/macosx/features/300.html). Apple Inc. 2008. . Retrieved June 13, 2008.

[96]   "Apple – BootCamp" (http://web.archive.org/web/20060602044022/http://www.apple.com/macosx/bootcamp/). Apple Inc. 2006. Archived from the original (http://www.apple.com/macosx/bootcamp/) on June 2, 2006. . Retrieved June 5, 2006.

[97]   "Mac OS X Leopard – Technology – UNIX" (http://www.apple.com/server/macosx/technology/unix.html). *Leopard Technology Overview*. Apple Inc. . Retrieved October 26, 2007. "Leopard is now an Open Brand UNIX 03 Registered Product, conforming to the SUSv3 and POSIX 1003.1 specifications for the C API, Shell Utilities, and Threads."

[98]   "Do Classic applications work with Mac OS X 10.5 or Intel-based Macs?" (http://docs.info.apple.com/article.html?artnum=303137). *Knowledge Base.* Apple Inc.. January 13, 2006. . Retrieved October 25, 2007.

[99]   "OS X Snow Leopard Hot News" (http://www.apple.com/macosx/snowleopard/?sr=hotnews). Apple Inc. June 9, 2008. . Retrieved June 10, 2008.

[100]   "Apple – Mac OS X – What is Mac OS X – Safari" (http://www.apple.com/macosx/what-is-macosx/safari.html). Apple Inc. October 22, 2009. . Retrieved October 22, 2009.

[101]   Lynch, Steven (June 12, 2008). "Mac OS X Snow Leopard Drops PowerPC Support" (http://www.hardocp.com/news/2008/06/11/snow_leopard_will_support_powerpcs). HardOCP. . Retrieved October 20, 2010.

[102]   Reisinger, Don (January 6, 2011). "Mac App Store launches on Snow Leopard" (http://news.cnet.com/8301-13506_3-20027548-17.html). CNET. .

[103]   "Apple – OS X Lion - The world's most advanced desktop operating system." (http://www.apple.com/macosx/lion/). Apple Inc. October 20, 2010. . Retrieved October 20, 2010.

External links

- Official website (http://www.apple.com/macosx/)
- Apple's listings of 3rd party software for Mac OS X (http://www.apple.com/downloads/)

Single-player video game

A **Single-player video game** is a video game where input from only one player is expected throughout the course of the gaming session. "Single-player game" usually implies a game that can only be played by one person, while "single-player mode" usually refers to a game mode for a single player, wherhe several players may play in a different mode.[1] The earliest video games, such as *Tennis for Two*, *Spacewar!*, and *Pong*, were two-player, with single-player games gaining popularity soon after with titles such as *Speed Race* and *Space Invaders*. In 1978, the first multiplayer role-playing games, known as MUDs, were created. The early 1990s introduced many games which utilized local area networks and null modems for multiplayer mode. *Doom* is a notable example of one such game.

The major selling points of larger single-player games are interesting storylines, impressive graphics, and realistic non-player characters and opponents. Notable examples include action-adventure games such as *The Legend of Zelda*, platform games such as *Mario* and *Sonic*, stealth games such as *Metal Gear*, survival horror such as *Resident Evil* and *Silent Hill*, and first-person shooters such as *Doom*, *Half-Life* and *Deus Ex*. Selling points of the smaller games are low learning curve and availability (many are free to play on various sites).

Certain game genres are inherently oriented towards single-player in their design. Such genres include puzzle games, such as *Tetris*, and plot-based role-playing games (RPGs), such as *Dragon Quest* and *Final Fantasy*. Recent additions to these genres, such as the massively multiplayer online games (MMOGs) or online multiplayer versions of *Tetris*, are serving to undo this trend.

The vast majority of modern console games and arcade games are designed so that they can be played by a single player; although many of these games have modes that allow two or more players to play (not necessarily simultaneously), very few actually require more than one player for the game to be played. The *Unreal Tournament* series is an example of such.

See also

- Multiplayer video game
- List of video gaming topics

References

[1] Oosterhuis, Kas; Feireiss, Lukas (March, 2006). *The Architecture Co-laboratory: Game Set and Match II : on Computer Games, Advanced Geometries, and Digital Technologies* (http://books.google.co.uk/books?id=tXBdOoZ-faYC&pg=RA2-PA108&dq=single+player+ simulations#PRA2-PA108,M1). Delft: Delft University of Technology. p. 180. ISBN 9059730364. .

Article Sources and Contributors

Penumbra: Overture *Source*: http://en.wikipedia.org/w/index.php?title=Penumbra:_Overture *Contributors*: A. Falcao, Acolyte of Discord, AderakConsteen, Anticipation of a New Lover's Arrival, The, Arthena, AxG, Burbble, Ced117, Chargh, Christoph hausner, Commander Shepard, Cronus91, Dachannien, Daeval, David Gerard, Eastgate, Eduemoni, Eik Corell, Elyscape, Enok, FAMAS, FoH, Folket, Frankenpuppy, Gazimoff, Geoff B, Goa103, GregorB, HDCase, Intgr, Itanius, JasonS2101, JayC, Jojje, Joylock, Koavf, Kocio, LOL, Lost on belmont, Lots42, Markdask, Martarius, Mdebets, Meegs, Methane is not water, Ntsimp, Plastikspork, Postwar, Ppntori, Retahnoitcerrochctip, Rjwilmsi, Schuitild, ShadowMan1od, Sharkface217, SkyWalker, SoloWing3844, Struenang, SuperGerbil, Tabletop, Tbhotch, TheCheesy4MkII, Timsheridan, Tjubert, Torchiest, Tsunami643, UKER, Urkle0, Will Xiu, Woohookitty, Óðinn, 71 anonymous edits

Graphic adventure game *Source*: http://en.wikipedia.org/w/index.php?title=Graphic_adventure_game *Contributors*: -5-, ADrakeIsl, AmericanLeMans, Certes, Cherkash, Cuvtixo, Darth Mike, Dina, Gbrading, Geniac, Grey ghost, Hahnchen, Ilsonowl, Jagged 85, Kannie, Keith D, LonelyMarble, Lord mortekai, Martarius, Megata Sanshiro, Merte123, Mika1h, Miremare, Mr. Siegal, N. Harmonik, Nbarth, OrangeDog, Prime Blue, Randomran, Rehevkor, Ruud Koot, Sada Abe, Salix alba, SharkD, Silver Edge, Skrapion, SkyWalker, TenPoundHammer, Th1rt3en, The Thing That Should Not Be, Thibbs, Thinhin of you, Valley2city, Vranak, Wood Thrush, X201, ΑΦΠ, 67 anonymous edits

Frictional Games *Source*: http://en.wikipedia.org/w/index.php?title=Frictional_Games *Contributors*: AlexiusHoratius, BD2412, Bped1985, Chargh, Christoph hausner, Coffee, Commander Shepard, Dreadstar, Hebrides, Hmains, JayC, Ke5ha93, Kenoxite, LOL, Logan, Manofmuchfailure, MeGustaTroll, Mika1h, MikeVitale, MuZemike, Pointillist, Shotalot, SkyWalker, Syrthiss, Tbhotch, Theregoesgravity, Threadnecromancer, Väsk, Wai0005, Óðinn, 46 anonymous edits

Penumbra: Requiem *Source*: http://en.wikipedia.org/w/index.php?title=Penumbra:_Requiem *Contributors*: Ainlina, Austriacus, Bovineboy2008, Chargh, Christoph hausner, DZ987, Daedalus969, Dawynn, Eik Corell, Geoff B, Glane23, Insectwarfare9999, Iohannes Animosus, Jagno, JasonS2101, JayC, Kevinkor2, Meeraq87, Mika1h, Miquonranger03, N. Harmonik, Plastikspork, Postwar, Retahnoitcerrochctip, Romanito, ScottSteiner, SkyWalker, Tabletop, Threadnecromancer, Trikkster, UKER, Óðinn, 64 anonymous edits

Microsoft Windows *Source*: http://en.wikipedia.org/w/index.php?title=Microsoft_Windows *Contributors*: -Majestic-, 03jmgibbens, 1(), 16@r, 1nt2, 2mcm, 2toy mora, 62.253.64.xxx, 67773732TYU, 68DANNY2, 9ms, A Raider Like Indiana, A gnome, A-giau, A7x, ACCOM2222, Abhishikt, AbsoluteFlatness, Academic Challenger, Acroterion, Adam Mirowski, Adamacious, Adamodell, Admin@pcrevs.com, Ae-a, Aeæ, Afro Article, Ageha Winds, Ahodacsek, Ahoerstemeier, Aidan W, Aido2002, Aihtdikh, AimalCool, Airplaneman, Ajm81, Akamad, Akhristov, Akira-otomo, Aksi great, Albert0057, Aldie, Alegoo92, Alemily, Alfio, AlistairMcMillan, Allstarecho, Almafeta, Alpha 4615, Alphathon, Alphius, Alshaheen15, Althepal, Am088, Amakuru, Amcfreely, Amrykid, Andre Engels, Andrevan, Andrewtechhelp, Andros 1337, Andy16666, Andyh2, Angeljon121, Ann Stouter, Anog, Anonymous Dissident, Anonymous56789, Antandrus, Anthall1991, Antimatter15, Antique Rose, Anville, Anþony, Aomarks, Aqair, Aranel, Arch dude, Archer3, Archivist, Aria1561, Arnoldkul, Arthena, Ashdurbat, AstroNomer, Astroview120mm, Aude, Audrius u, AussieLegend, AvantgardeMVC, Aveilleux, Avenue, Avihut, Avocado27, Ayjay1545, Azrael Nightwalker, B, BNSF Man, BUzTeD, Badwolf2212, Bakery2k, Banes, Barek, Barrera marquez, Bartosz, Bbq man, Bbriggs1, Bdoserror, Bdshort1, Beao, Beinsane, Ben-Zin, Benandorsqueaks, Benc, Berek, Bergsten, Betelgeuse, Bevo, Bhadani, Bibliomaniac15, Big Bird, Big Booger, BigCow, BillG, BillWSmithJr, Billyswong, Bimmerosx, Binsurf, Binzisimpsons, Bissinger, Blackanddarkness, Blackcap95, Blackcats, Blakkandekka, Blaxthos, Bleakcomb, Blobglob, Blowdart, Blubberboy92, BlueCaper, Blueforce4116, Bluestriker, Bo98, Bobo192, Bobwrit, Bogods, Bollyjeff, Boris Allen, BostonMA, Boylett, Brandizzi, Brandon Brown, Brian0918, BrianGo28, BrianRecchia, Brianski, Brisvegas, BrokenSegue, Bubba hotep, Buchanan-Hermit, Buddha24, Bunnyhop11, Burntsauce, CRFWNY, CWenger, Cacophony, Cadiomals, Caffelice, Caltas, Camembert, Can't sleep, clown will eat me, Canadian-Bacon, Candamir, Candorwien, CanisRufus, Caper13, CaptainVindaloo, Casper10, Casper2k3, Cayindra, Cbrown1023, Cburnett, Ceeon, Celestra, CesarB, Ceyockey, Cff12345, Cgnabod, Cgs, Charles Gaudette, Charles dye, Chazz, Cherkash, Chille, Chmpoure, Chocolatemilk94, Chowbok, Chris 73, Chris Pickett, Chris the speller, Christian List, Chriswoz, Ciao 90, CitronManden, Cityscape4, Cjcamilla, Cjordan93, ClamDip, ClockworkTroll, Cncccer, Cncxbox, Codificate, Codyblevins, Coffee, Colejohnson66, Colin Hill, Cometstyles, Commander Keane, Computer boy2, Computerdan000, ConCompS, Coniosis, Conman23456, Conversion script, Coolcaesar, CoolingGibbon, Corporal clegg48, Courcelles, Cp111, Cpiral, Crazycomputers, Crazyromo, Crem23, Cremepuff222, Cristan, Crpietschmann, Cryptic, Cstanners, Ctbolt, Cuvtixo, Cvinoth, Cwolfsheep, Cyktsui, Cynical, Darthnader37, Dasani, DataMatrix, Databases, Davelane, David Biddulph, David Gerard, David1409, Davidjk, Dcandeto, Dcolvin, Deanhowell123, Debackerl, December21st2012Freak, Deeahbz, Dehumanizer, Delirium, Delldot, Deltabeignet, Demmy, Denniss, Derek Parnell, Deryck Chan, Dethomas, Deus2, Dieboybun, Diegogrez, DigbyDalton, Digita, DigitalLife, Dimre01, Dina, Dinhtuydzao, Dinjired, Dinnerface, DinosaursLoveExistence, Disorganisation Man, Dj789, Djegan, Djhybrid117, Djmasala, Dmerrill, DmitryKo, Dog1818, Dojarca, Dolphinn, Downloaddude1258, Dp462090, Dragar Gt, Dragon 280, DragonflySixtyseven, Dragonhelmuk, Dstln, Dtech, Dudesleeper, Dungodung, Dust Filter, Dustin gayler, Dwheeler, Dylan Flaherty, Dysprosia, Dzubint, EH74DK, Eagleal, Ed g2s, Edgar181, Edgarde, EdgeOfEpsilon, Eelamstylez77, Eggsacute, Egil, Eivindsol, El Dominio, Elassint, Eliotwiki, ElliotAdderton, Ellmist, Elm-39, Eloquence, Elwood00, Emacsuser, Enco1984, Endofskull, Enigmaaaaa, Enno, Enochlau, Ente75, Eraserhead1, Ergosteur, Esanchez7587, Escape Orbit, Esebi95, Evice, Evil Monkey, Evil saltine, Evosoho, Ewlyahoocom, Exodite, F80, FF2010, Fabsss, Faisal.akeel, Faithlessthewonderboy, Falco McCloud, Fantasy, Faradayplank, FatalError, Fatjoe151, Favonian, FayssalF, Fbv65edel, Fdp, Felipe Aira, Ferkelparade, Ffx, Fiskegalen92, Fitzebwoy, Fiver2552, Flamurai, Flanakin, FleetCommand, Flying Bishop, FlyingPenguins, Foo1995, Fowl2, FrancoGG, Frap, Fraslet, Freakofnurture, Frecklefoot, Fred Bradstadt, Frederik.Questier, FreeKresge, Freeeekyyy, Frenchman113, FreplySpang, FrozenPurpleCube, Frozenport, Fuck You, Funandtrvl, Furrykef, Fuzheado, GDonato, GNUtoo, GSK, Gabrielpokemon, Gadfium, Gaius Cornelius, Galactor213, Galoubet, Galwhaa, GamerXp, Gamerzworld, Gaming&Computing, Ganeshotaku, Ganfon, Gang65, Gaodifan, Gardar Rurak, Gary King, Gary Kirk, Gavin.perch, Gazpacho, Ged UK, Geek45, Geoffspear, George Adam Horváth, Georgia guy, Geraki, Gerbrant, Ghettoblaster, Gilbertogm, Gilliam, Glen, Gnepets, Goatasaur, Gobonobo, Gogo Dodo, Goldom, Googler459, Googlesucks56789, Gosub, Graham87, GrandPoohBah, Grayshi, Grin, Grm wnr, Groggy Dice, Gronky, Grunt, Gryllida, Gscshoyru, Gtdp, Gunnar Guðvarðarson, Gustyfalcon, Guy Harris, Guyjohnston, HJ Mitchell, Haakon, Haeleth, Hahafatpeople, Hairchrm, Hall Monitor, Halsteadk, Hammersoft, Harryboyles, Hase09999, Hbomb phd mom, Hdt83, Heapchk, Hebrides, Helixblue, Hello32020, Hendrixski, Henry W. Schmitt, HereToHelp, Hirosho, Holbred, Howardjp, Hungupbg, Hurtstotalktoyou, Husky, Hydr, Hypnoticcyst, I have wood, I8189720, IGod, ILOVELOL32, IMSoP, IXella007, Iain99, Ialsoagree, Ian Pitchford, Ianjones50, Ichangefacts, Ilaiho, Illegal Operation, Illyria05, Ilya, IlyaHaykinson, Ilyanep, Indefatigable, Indon, Injust, Interframe, Ioprwe, Ipodsocool, Iridescent, IsUsername, ItsProgrammable, Ivan Pozdeev, Ixfd64, J Di, J36miles, JCarriker, JIP, JLaTondre, JWSchmidt, JYOuyang, JYolkowski, Jacob Hnri 5, JacquesStrap, Jaericho, Jake Wasdin, Jamieostrich, Jan Hofmann, Jasper Deng, Jauerback, Jaxl, Jcbparry, Jcurtin, Jdlowery, Jdm64, Jeffwang, Jeh, Jennie--x, Jeremy Visser, JeremyA, Jerryseinfeld, Jerrysmp, Jesse Viviano, Jesus5555, Jesus764, Jesuss, JettaMann, Jevel66, Jiffy, Jigs41793, Jimmi Hugh, Jimothytrotter, Jimthing, Jiy, Jketola, Jkonline, Jmath666, Jmjglick, Jmoynihan08hm77, JoJan, JoThousand, Joanjoc, JoanneB, Joe2832, Joejoejo, Joffeloff, Johann Wolfgang, John, John Ericson, John Goettle, John Quincy Adding Machine, JohnJamesWilson, JohnOwens, Johnclow13, Johnleemk, Johnmc, Johnuniq, Jojit fb, Jon vs, JonasL, Jonatan Swift, Jondel, Jonghyunchung, Jopxton, Jordan015, Jordanyoung17, Jose Concepcion, Josh the Nerd, Joshua Issac, JoshuaArgent, Joyous!, Jpoke89, Jrcure, Jsmethers, Jtc, Ju6613r, JuJube, JuanC08, Julian Mendez, Jumbo Snails, Justanother, Jyoz, Kakomu, Kar.ma, Karimarie, Karlo2002, Karnesky, Katarighe, Kaycubs, Kaysov, Kbh3rd, Kbolino, Kelly Martin, Kenny Strawn, Kesla, Kevinkor2, Keyser Söze, Khym Chanur, Kierenj, Kigali1, KingpinE7, Kinneyboy90, Kipholbeck, Kissmeplease, Kittyhawk2, Kklowa, Kkm010, Klingoncowboy4, KnowledgeOfSelf, Knutux, Kohlmalo, Kolonuk, Koman90, Kop, Korossyl, Kozuch, KrakatoaKatie, Krawi, KrisBogdanov, Kungfuadam, Kungming2, Kurieeto, Kwen, Kypr8, L Kensington, La goutte de pluie, Lacrimosus, Lahiru k, Lantay77, Larry laptop, Lbs6380, Lcarsdata, Lead$peaker, Leandrod, Lectonar, LeeHunter, Leif, Leithp, LeoNomis, Letdorf, Leuko, Liberty Miller, Lightmouse, Linear88, Linuxbeak, Linuxerist, LionKimbro, Llalala, Localzuk, Loismum, Lonaowna, LonelyBeacon, Looksliketrent, Lord British, Lordalpha1, Lotje, Lou.weird, Lowellian, Luce007, Luk, Lumpbucket, Luna Santin, Lupin, M Johnson, MADCastro2012, MCC, MER-C, MERC, MJ94, MJGR, MK8, MMMEEE, MZMcBride, Ma8thew, Mac, MacGeekGuy, Macurry, Madcow 93, Maester mensch, Magister Mathematicae, Mailer diablo, MainFrame, Malo, Man123123, Marceki111, Marcok, Mark, Mark85296341, MarkGallagher, MarkSpearmint, Markhurd, Markie2, Markustwofour, Martarius, Martyx, Marudubshinki, Marx Gomes, Marysunshine, Massysett, MasterCole, Mastershake86, Mathwizxp, Matt Crypto, Matt.forestpath, MattGiuca, Mattarata, Mav, Max Schwarz, Maxim Masiutin, Maximus Rex, McLovin34, Mcwatson, Meelar, Mehran, Mephiles602, Metalim, Methanegas, Metz2000, Mguy77, Mgw854, Michael Angelkovich, Michael Ray, Michaeldadmum, Michaelpremsrirat, MichealH, Midgrid, Midkay, Mike4ty4, MikeZuniga, Mild Bill Hiccup, Milfman, Minesweeper, MinorItem, Miros 0571, Mithent, Mjpieters, Mkdw, Mlscdi, Mmoll21m, Mmoller, Mms, Mo0, Modster, Mokk123, Monedula, Monothleft, MontyB, Moonknightus, Moonridersaregay, Moonwolf14, Mr Bartels, Mr. Lefty, Mr. XYZ, Mrdelayer, Mrleewilliams, Ms2ger, Mugunth Kumar, Mulad, Mushroom, Mvmarier, Mwtoews, Mxn, Myanw, Nachmore, Naddy, Naltrexone, Nanshu, NapoliRoma, Nathan nfm, Nathanlilienthal13, Neckername, Neelchauhan, Neo The User, Neo2256, NewGuy4, Newfraferz87, Nicholas Love, Nick2253, Nickenzi, Nimc, Nintendog master 54, Nishkid64, Nixdorf, Njan, Nmnmnm, Noypi380, Nukleartoaster, Nurg, O, Odd bloke, Off!, Okwestern, OlEnglish, Olioster, Ollie the Magic Skater, Omicronpersei8, Ondrejsv, Oneupthextraman, Opagecrtr, Opelio, OregonD00d, Oscarthecat, Ost316, OtherPerson, OwenX, Oxymoron83, Ozherb, PPGMD, Packard Bell Legend, Padsquad43, Pakaran, Patrick, Patrickweeks007, Patrolman89, Paul Stansifer, Paulfp, Pavel Vozenilek, Persian Poet Gal, Person1936, Petaluma Paranormal, Peter Grey, Peteturtle, Petrwiki, Peyman4u, Peyre, Pgiii, Pgk, Phanton, Phil Sandifer, Philip Trueman, Phoogenb, Pigman, PileOnades, Pinikas, Piratesmack, Plugwash, PoWwOw123, Pokyrek, Poor Yorick, Poweroid, Prolog, Propound, Pschulz01, PsyMar, Puffin, Pursey, QUAZWRATH, Qantasplanes, Qudder, Quinsareth, Quoladdie, Qwerty124gg, Qwitchibo, Qxl32, Qxz, R'n'B, RB972, RTC, RadioActive, RadioFan, Radon210, Raja99, Ramanpotential, RandomP, Rasmasyean, Rbuj, Rchamberlain, Rcmouse1010, Rd syringe, Rderijcke, Rdsmith4, Reallikeunreal, Rebecca, Rebroad, Red Dalek, Red Director, RedKlonoa, RedXII, Redvers, Reilly, Reisio, Remember the dot, Repetition, Resplendent, RevolverOcelotX, Rgbc2000, Rhesusmonkeyboy, Rhobite, Rhtc, Rich Farmbrough, Richard Lotspard, Richard626, Ricjl, RickK, Riluve, Rincewind32, Rjecina, Rjwilmsi, Rl, Robartin, Robbie940, Robert Bisset, Robert H, Robert Xia, RobertG, Robertd, Robinhw, Rocastelo, Rocket71048576, Rockymountains, Rodeo90, Roketjack, RolandH, Ronark, Rsantmann, Rsm99833, Running, Rursus, Rutherfordjigsaw, Ruud Koot, Rwwww, Ryan Norton, Ryan Postlethwaite, Ryan t moua, S0aasdf2sf, SF007, SHARD, SHeumann, SNIyer12, ST47, SYSS Mouse, Sae1962, Sam Hocevar, Samuel, Samuel Blanning, Samvscat, Sango123, Sasquatch, Sauronjim, Scepia, SchmuckyTheCat, SchuminWeb, Science4sail, Scientus, Scifiintel, Sciurinæ, Scorpiona, Scottymoze, Scriberius, Scuiqui fox, SeanMack, Sebmathews, Sebrat, Secretlondon, Selfdiscipline, Selivanow, September 11 terrorist, Sethoeph, Sfan00 IMG, Shadowfyren, Shadowjams, Shakumafu, Shandris, Shanes, Shashank Shekhar, Shelmac, Sherylanne, Shibboleth, Shinjiman, Shnout, Sigma 7, Sigmundpetersen, Siskin, Silvergoat, SimonEast, SimonP, SimonTrew, Simple Bob, Simxp, SirGrant, Siroxo, Sjakkalle, Sjorford, Skirks, Skiwi, Skyeap, Slashuer, Slathering, Sleepeeg3, Slipknotmetal, SmackEater, Smokizzy, SmoothNikola, Smurfy, Smyth, Snaxe920, Snoyes, SoSaysChappy, Solphusion, Somaditya, Somebody in the WWW, Soumyasch, SouthernNights, Southpark20, Spe88, Spear of fire, SpecMode, Specter01010, SpeedyGonsales, Spencerperry, Sperling, Spliced, Spookfish, Spug, Srnelson, Ssd, Starionwolf, Steel, Steezly, StephenH, Stephenchou0722, Stevenh123, Stevenmitchell, Stevietheman, Stilroc, Stino v, Stonda, StuIsCool, StuThomas, Supercooljs2, Supers, Supremeknowledge, Suruena, SusanLesch, Susvolans, Swabjob, Sweetback, Swollib, Swotboy2000, SyntaxError55, Syrthiss, Szhang21, TAG.Odessa, TJ Spyke, Ta bu shi da yu, Tacvek,

Tadas12, TakuyaMurata, Tangotango, Tannin, Tarashav, Tawker, Tbhotch, Teamcritical, Tech2blog, Techman224, Techmdrn, Template namespace initialisation script, Tepidpond, Terence, Tfgbd, Thaek, Thalakan, Thavian, The Colclough, The Disco Times, The Epopt, The Fish, The Geneticist, The Rambling Man, The wub, TheChrisD, TheDoober, TheGeneralUser, TheKMan, TheNewPhobia, ThePointblank, Thealexweb, Theazman1, Thegreenj, Thetehror, Thewallowmaker, Thewikipedian, Thingg, Think outside the box, This, that and the other, Thisisntfake1, Thomas Larsen, Thompson.matthew, Thorpe, Throup, Thu, Thumperward, TiCPU, Tiggerjay, TimR, Timberframe, Timmeh, Timwi, Tinton5, ToasterOS, Tom Morris, Tomcage9, Tommy Irianto, Tompagenet, Tomy9510, Tonsofpcs, Tony1, Tothwolf, Towel401, Towsonu2003, Toyotaboy95, Tracer9999, Train2104, Treekids, Tregoweth, TrekMaster, Trevor MacInnis, Tripacer99, Trivialist, Trusilver, Tsunaminoai, Ttwaring, TubularWorld, TuneyLoon, Turionaltec, TuukkaH, Twernt, Twickline, Tyomitch, Tyraios, Tyrol5, UMC2, Uli, Ultimus, Umofomia, Unimaginative Username, Unknownperson1234, Uriel8, Utcursch, Vahid83, Valenciano, Vanished 6551232, Vbrtrmn, Vedek Dukat, Vegaswikian, Vincent.premysler, Vontafeijos, Vrenator, W1 m2, Wackymacs, Walter Görlitz, WalterGR, Wanderson9, Wangmike, Wapcaplet, Warlordwolf, Warren, Weararedjacket, Wengier, Werdan7, Werideatdusk33, Westley Turner, Whiteford8, Whkoh, Widefox, Wiki alf, Wiki fanatic, WikiBone, WikiFew, WikiMan44, Wikidexel2, Wikinger, WikipedianMarlith, Wikiwaka101, Windowsknowitall@msn.com, WindowzRULZlolZ, Windsok, Wknight94, Wlklpedla is meant to be vandalized, Wmahan, Wmplayer, Woohookitty, Wow1000, Wragge, Wsoder, Wykis, X1987x, XJamRastafire, Xation, Xelgen, Xeysz, Xgmx, Ximian99, Xlation, Xmachina, Xp54321, Xpclient, XrXeJoeXaXpXeXr, Xtreme racer, Xxglennxx, YUL89YYZ, Yama, Yamamoto Ichiro, Yamla, Yasirniazkhan, Yeeshenhao, Yergizmo, Ynhockey, Yousifnet, Yuckfoo, Yuhong, Z.E.R.O., Z98, ZFU738, Zakfleming, ZamorakO o, Zapvet, Zeeboid, Zepheus, Zer0431, Zntrip, Zondor, Zoney, Zundark, , , , 1542 anonymous edits

Penumbra: Black Plague *Source*: http://en.wikipedia.org/w/index.php?title=Penumbra:_Black_Plague *Contributors*: Acolyte of Discord, Astroview120mm, Chargh, Christoph hausner, Clubby the Seal, Commander Shepard, Cyclonius, Darklilac, Deor, Diannaa, DragonSpawn343, Eik Corell, Elockid, FoH, Geoff B, GoingBatty, GrizzlyGar, Gruverja, Hanchi, Itanius, Jaro7788, JasonS2101, JayC, Joylock, Lamro, Legitimus, MagnusGuyra, Mateuszzz88, Meaghan, Meeraq87, Mika1h, Miuq, Nalatkal, NellieBly, Plastikspork, Postwar, PseudoOne, RGMing, Retahnoitcerrochctip, Rheadild, SkyWalker, Streeshet, Tbhotch, Tjubert, Tony Sidaway, UKER, Urkle0, Vianello, Welsh, X201, Óðinn, 63 anonymous edits

Mac OS X *Source*: http://en.wikipedia.org/w/index.php?title=Mac_OS_X *Contributors*: !Darkfire!6'28'14, 108.00a, 1manfern, 209.75.42.xxx, 3velvet3, 475Michael, 4piecemcnugget, 5 albert square, A plague of rainbows, A3RO, A8UDI, ACupOfCoffee, AGK, AGiorgio08, ATravelingGeek, Aamanliguez, Aanhorn, AaronSw, Abce2, Abevacqua, Achalkley, Adam2288, AdamAtlas, Adashiel, Adjusting, AdmN, Aeons, After Midnight, Ahodes1, Ahoerstemeier, Aido2002, Airplaneman, Ais523, Aisha9152, Aitias, Aj800, Ajclayton, Akcarver, Akhristov, Alan De Smet, Alba, Alegoo92, Alex.muller, Alex43223, AlexanderHaas, Alexibu, AlistairMcMillan, Alixioa, AlloOO2, Althepal, Anarcho hipster, Andre Engels, AndrewHowse, AndrewLovesComputing, Andy M. Wang, Andyluciano, Anetode, Angelic Wraith, Animum, Anonymous Dissident, Ant, Antandrus, AntiOnline, Antonio Lopez, Apokrif, Apple1976, Applecot, Applemeister, Archivist, AriX, ArielGold, Armandeh, Artaxiad, Asparagus, Atlant, AussieLegend, Austin512, Avalys, Avenged Eightfold, BD2412, BENJAS SR, Baa, Bad ideas, Bailey7677, Barefootguru, Barek, Barras, Barticus88, Baryonic Being, Bbarsh, Bbatsell, Bdesham, Beatlesfan2087, Beaulieugang, Beginnersview, Beland, Bencey, Beno1000, Bentorr, Bill4927, BillSkosh3, Billgatesass, Bissinger, Bivalve, Bizzarefoods, Bla1122, BlackDeath3, Blacksilk8, Blanchardb, Blastfamy, Bluefusion, Bluerasberry, Bmike8, Boarder8925, Bob12345678987654321, Bobblewik, Bobdobbs1723, Bobnorwal, Bobo192, Bodnotbod, Bojan, Boney9801, Bongwarrior, Boredzo, Brainix, Brandon, Brent27, Brian Kendig, Briancollins, Brianreading, Brion VIBBER, BrowserWARwarning, Brycen, Btm, Bubba hotep, Bubba73, Bugman, Bushing, Butterfly0fdoom, Byrial, CD-Host, CL8, Cacepi, Calmer Waters, Calor, Caltas, Cameron.g.brown, Campesr, Can't sleep, clown will eat me, CanadianLinuxUser, CanisRufus, Cantus, Canwolf, Capricorn42, CardinalFangZERO, CarrerCrytharis, Casconed, Caseybutt, Catwhoorg, CecilWard, Cennin, Cesarojedac, Ceyockey, Chairman S., Chamal N, Chaosbunny, Charles Gaudette, Charleschuck, Chealer, Cherkash, Chmod 777, Chmod007, Chrisplyon, Chun-hian, Ciaccona, CieloEstrellado, Cjcid, Clairesstone, Cleared as filed, Closedmouth, CloudStrife, Cobi, Coffee, Colejohnson66, Colonels1020, Columbia747, ConMan, Coniosis, Conman23456, Conti, Conversion script, CoolFox, CoolingGibbon, Corbin Benton Davenport, Corcyn, Corpx, Corti, Cowguru2000, Cpiral, Craigdnorris, Cransdell, CrazyTerabyte, Crazypush planyour..., Crownjewel82, Ctachme, Ctrlfreak13, CunningWizard, Cvkline, Cws125, CyberSkull, Cybercat, Cybercobra, Cyclopia, Cyktsui, Cylauj, Cyrius, DMCer, DMacks, Dagibit, Dair Grant, Dakoman, Dale Arnett, Damian Yerrick, Damieng, Danbt79, Danlev, Darkov, Darkyeffectt, Darrien, David Fell, David Gerard, David Latapie, David Rudnick, Davidfstr, Davidmarkman, Daytonlowell, Dbfirs, Dchall1, DeTru711, Debresser, Deeahbz, Deflective, Delirium, Delldot, DerHexer, Derfbwh, Destin, Dethelf, Deus Ex, Dgrant, Didacticderivative, Diggins24, DirkZöttl, Dismas, Diverman, Djg2006, Djsasso, DocWatson42, Donfbreed, Donreed, Doodledoo, Dr Fell, Dragon76, Drakino, Dratman, Dravick, Dremie, Driftingaway, Drockius, DropDeadGorgias, Dspradau, Duke53, Dysprosia, Dystopianray, EEMIV, EJSawyer, EagleOne, EddEdmondson, Eddpayne, EdgeOfEpsilon, EdoDodo, Eeinfo2008, Eequor, Eggybacon, Ego Tripper, Ehurtley, Eitch, Elektrik Shoos, Elfguy, Eliah, Elipongo, Ellmist, Elsendero, Emmelie, EmpMac, Emre D., EngineerScotty, Enviroboy, EonOmega, Epastore, Epbr123, Ephilei, EqualRights, Eraserhead1, EricNau, Ericlewis91, Erik Swanson, Errantminion, Esanchez7587, Escape Orbit, Esebi95, Esheldon, Esrever, EugeneZelenko, EvelinaB, Evice, Evil Merlin, Evil saltine, EvilChemist, Evildeathmath, Excirial, Ezekielelin, FF2010, FMAN, FP.DBZ, Faith healer, Falcon9x5, Fdgdf3, Felixthomas, FeralDruid, Ferdinand h2, Fetchcomms, Ffiti, FightingStreet, Finn mccool, Finny388, Fireball1244, Fish and karate, FlamingSilmaril, FlashSheridan, Flewis, Fligabob, Flimsyq, Flyguy649, Flyingember, Foosh, For great justice., Forlornturtle, Fran z, Frankie0607, Frap, Fratrep, FrenchIsAwesome, Froth, Frungi, Func, Furrybeagle, Furrykef, Future Perfect at Sunrise, Fuzheado, GRAHAMUK, Gaius Cornelius, Ganymede 901, Gardar Rurak, Gary King, Geniac, Gerbrant, Ghepeu, Ghettoblaster, Gifflite, Gjd001, Glyoma, Godlord2, GoldRenet, Gongfarmerzed, Good Olfactory, Goodolclint, Goose, Gorgeshrinks, Graham87, Grm wnr, Groink, Grstain, Grunt, Gu1dry, Guaka, Gurch, Gurchzilla, Guy Harris, Guyjohnston, Gwern, Gwernol, H2g2bob, HPSCHD, Hadal, Hadger, Haemo, Hairchrm, Haiviet, Hamiltondaniel, Hamtechperson, HangingCurve, Happywaffle, Harry the Dirty Dog, HarryP2511, Harryboyles, Haseo9999, Hateless, Havok, Hawaiian717, Hayabusa future, Haysead, HeffeQue, Heimstern, Helix84, Hello. I'm new here, but I'm sure I can help out., Hephaestos, Heracles31, Herbythyme, HereToHelp, Herr von underpants, Hervegirod, Hetar, Hfastedge, Hihellohow, Hmrox, Hn, Hohohob, Honta, Horrorshowlolk, Horserice, HoserHead, HowardBerry, Hrs himavanth, Hugh da pu, Humble Guy, Hut 8.5, HuwPrestatyn, Huwjones7, Huwr, Hvn0413, Hyad, Hydrogen Iodide, I didn't push her, I5bala, IMSoP, INic, INkubusse, Iancarter, Iccdel, Iliank, Ilikeapple, Illinois2011, Iluvcapra, InfinityAndBeyond, Ino5hiro, Inspe, Instigate cjsc (Narine), Invalidname, Ioapetraka, Iridescent, IslandGyrl, Ispy1981, Itaiyz97, Ithizar, Iuhkjhk87y678, J Di, J. Telmot, J.delanoy, Jaavaaguru, Jab843, Jack Merridew, Jack The Hat, Jackster, Jacobolus, Jacono, Jagislaqroo, JamieS93, Jammerpunk1089, JanusK, Jaredpr93, Jareha, Jarry1250, Jason C.K., JasonAQuest, Jasonfb, Jayshao, Jcarroll, Jclemens, Jearil, Jeff3000, Jeltz, Jennavecia, Jerebin, JeremyA, Jfliu, Jglyon, Jharrell, Jhdezjr, Jimthing, Jkh, Jmcgarey, Jnorton7558, JoeCool59, Joetexaco, John John 216, John254, JohnDBuell, JohnHWiki, Johnmarkos, Jolb, Jonabbey, Jonathanvt, Jordandanford, Jose Concepcion, Josh the Nerd, Joshschr, Jossi, Jovianeye, Jreem raddng, Jsephton, Jstupple7, Jtbean, Jtkiefer, Juancnuno, Julesd, Juliancolton, Justalex, Justpetehere, Jwisser, K95, K;;m5m k;;m5m, KAMiKAZOW, KC Panchal, Karl-Henner, Katalaveno, Kaztec, Kb9wte, Kbolino, Kdmurray, Keep-peer, KelleyCook, Kenirwin, Keraunoscopia, Ketiltrout, Keyser Söze, KhrOn0s, Kilowattradio, Kinema, Kinzera, Kirbytime, Kjngjkn, Kkm010, Klausness, Kmg90, Knowhands enjoykeep, KnowledgeOfSelf, Knubamboo, Knutux, Koavf, Kocio, Kodster, Kohlmalo, Kostas.karachalios, Koweja, Kozuch, Krellis, Kricxjo, Kungfuadam, Kunming2, Kwamikagami, Kylalak, Kylet, Kylu, Kyoko, LAX, LERK, LOL, Languagegeek, Latitudinarian, Laurinavicius, LeftClicker, Lennartgoosens, Lensi, Lensovet, Lethe, Lexlex, Lg 787, Lhasapso, Libertyforall1776, Liftarn, Lights, Lijijinaraj, Livedtype proveyourhuman gainsbreak fgn, Logixoul, Lorductape, LorenzoB, Lot49a, Lotje, Lovibond, LukeyBoy, Lupin, Lupo, Luxiake, Lysdexia, M.O.X, M1ss1ontomars2k4, MER-C, MFNickster, Maacquin, Mabdul, Mac OS X Critic, Mac maniac394, Macfan93, Macguy815, Macman213, Macslacker, Maester mensch, Magnesium, Magnus.de, Makaristos, Malikitiki, Malleus Fatuorum, Malthe Risager, ManfrenjenStJohn, Marcok, Mardus, Mariano Anto Bruno Mascarenhas, Mark.P.Bartlett, Marknews, Marko75, Markus451, Martarius, Materialscientist, Mathisreallycool, Mathrick, Mathwiz777, Matt Peacock, Mattbr, Mattworld, Maury Markowitz, Maustrauser, Max Naylor, Max Schwarz, Max.goedjen, Maxmasnick, Mdnky, Me6620, Mecki78, Mediaholic, Mediaright, MegaPedant, Melvin.chien, Memex, Mentifisto, Meow, Mernen, Merphant, Micahmn, Michael Fonfara, Mijio, Mike Fikes, Mike1, MikeCapone, Mikedotnet, Mikenolte, Milan Keršláger, Mild Bill Hiccup, Miles, Mindmatrix, Minghong, Ministry of Truth, Minno72, MinuteHand, MinutiaeMan, Miros 0571, Miskin, Mms, Moabdave, Monkfishbandana, Mono, Mortense, Mr.bombo, Mralston, Mrmaroon25, Mryoruichi, Mu5ti, Mugunth Kumar, Muhaidib, Muhandis, Muro de Aguas, Mushroom, Musser, Mutchy126, MuzikJunky, Mysterbrody, Mysterioususer, Mütze, NJA, Nakon, Nandesuka, Naryathegreat, Nathanblack12345, Nathanl1192, Navstar, NawlinWiki, NeoSchu, Nchaimov, Neilc, NerdyScienceDude, Nessup, Netsnipe, Newkai, Niceguysox, Nigelj, Nightscream, Nihiltres, Nikai, Nil Einne, Nimakha, Niro87, Nivix, Nohat, Non-dropframe, Northgrove, Notheruser, NuclearWarfare, Nunh-huh, ONEder Boy, Obsoletepower, Odie5533, Off we go, Ohconfucius, Oknazevad, Oleg Alexandrov, OliverOliverOliver, Oliverkroll, On2see, Onco p53, One, Oneiros, Onekopaka, Oneliketadow, Oneupthextraman, Oo7565, Openbsd00d, Orderud, OriginalGamer, Orphic, Ortolan88, Oscarthecat, Osxadvocate, Otsel7, Oxymoron83, PCRevs, Plrish, PRRfan, Padinc, Palaeozoic99, Palthrow, Pantergraph, Paradoxian, Paranoid, Paul 012, Paul-L, Paulirwin, Pax:Vobiscum, Pclover, Peachpittv, Pencilcase123, Petaluma Paranormal, PeterKz, PeterSymonds, Peteturtle, Pethr, Pewtermoose, Pgan002, PhilipB, Philwelch, Phobos11, Photar, Photographerguy, Piano non troppo, Pingswept, Pixelperfect777, Pjamescowie, Plop, Pokoleo, Pol098, Polarlys, Polluks, Porqin, Postdlf, Pownerus, Ppapasai, Pretzels, Prickus, Profoss, Prometheusg, Prowikipedians, Psantora, Ptomes, PyroGamer, Pyroflames0, Pzh777, Qaovxtazypdl, Qst, Quabblestick, Quasipalm, Quiddity, Qwe, Qxz, RMDRDR, RScheiber, RTC, Raekwon, Ramallite, RandalSchwartz, Rasmasyean, Raul654, Rawlogic, Raysonho, Rbuj, Reactor12, Rebroad, Robert P. O'Shea, Robertjm, Robertsmith6, Robzz, Rockeywood, Rogerd, Roguegeek, Rokaszil, Ronabop, Ronhjones, Rorschach, Rory O'Kane, Rosedaddy, Rosnh, Rostz, Rubberkeith, Runtime, Rwwww, Ryan Norton, Ryanlungdb, Rzęsor, S.Örvarr.S, SBuchholtz, SF007, SJP, SMC1991, SSTwinrova, STrRedWolf, Sai2020, Saint-Paddy, Sakurambo, Salocin, Sam Blacketer, Samballance, Samsara, Samwb123, Sannse, Saxsux, Scaredpoet, Schissel, Schneelocke, Scott Wilson, Sdalmonte, Sdfisher, Sdneidich, Sean Gray, Seanny22, Seansinc, Seiche, Seth Nimbosa, Seth ze, Sfacets, Sg09836, Shadowradiance, ShaneCavanaugh, Shanel, ShaunL, Sherkhon, SiPlus, Sigma 7, SimX, Simetrical, Simharrison, Simulcra, SirMetal, Sk8rSoda, Skedaddle, SkyWalker, Skybon, SkydiveMike, Slp1, Slyguy, Smacdonald, Snarius, SnetskyCM, Snowolf, SoWhy, Soliloquial, Sophisticated 23, Soulhack, Soumyasch, Sp0ken4, Spacepotato, Speer320, Spellcast, Sphivo, Splateagle, Spobbs, Sproject, SpuriousQ, Sputnik 99, Squash, Sr Dude, Stan Shebs, Stardotboy, Stealth500, Stephan Leeds, Stephen Shaw, Stephenchou0722, SterlingNorth, Steve Zerr, Stevekinn, Stevenrasnick, Stevesy, Stormwatch, Stroppolo, Stuhacking, Suduser85, Sukiari, Supasaru, Surv1v4l1st, Suspie, Sverdrup, Swany1012, Swaq, Swebert, Sweets, Synchronism, Syp, T.O. Rainy Day, T.roome, TCorp, TDS, TUF-KAT, Tanvir Ahmmed, Tarquin, Tblackma222, Tbsdy lives, TeaDrinker, Tech30, Techman224, Terhorstj, Terrillja, Th1rt3en, ThatPeskyCommoner, Thaurisil, The Evil IP address, The Fish, The Halo, The Thing That Should Not Be, The twizz, TheDataMonster, TheProject, TheSameGuy, TheWama, Theanthrope, Thedeakinator, Thg250, Thomas Gilling, ThomasHarte, Thoshijima, Thumperward, Tiger 10.4, TigerK 69, TigerShark, Tigeron, TijhofGraphics, Tiki2099, Tim R, Tippx, Tizio, Tjoneslo, Tmuller2, Tommy Kronkvist, Tommy2010, Tomwins76, Tony1, Topbanana, Tothwolf, Tpavra, Tranceraph, Travishorrell, Trbdavies, Tree Falling In The Forest, Trendyhendy, TrevorLSciAct, Trevyn, TreyHarris, Triona, Tristanb, Triwbe, Tslag, TubularWorld, Turian, Turkey0918, TutterMouse, TuukkaH, Tverbeek, Tweisbach, Typhoon, UkPaolo, Ultimate753, Uniquely Fabricated, Unixfanatic, Unsungheroz83, Urpunkt, Utcursch, Utkarsh apple, V-train, Validbanks 34, Vansunder, VasilievVV, Vbdrummer0, Verloren, Versus22, Vespristiano, VladGenie, Volanaro, Vollex, Wackymacs, Waggers, Walafrid, Wannger27, Warmfuzzygrrl, Warren, Wattyirl, Wavelength, Wayward, WazzaMan, Wcquidditch, Wei.cs, Welsh, Wernher, Whaleyland, Whayworth, Whkoh, WikiHead, Wiki Raja, Wiki alf, Wikievil666, Wikinerd20, WikipedianMarlith, Wiknerd, Wildthing61476, Will Beback, Wingedbunny1, Wittylama, Woohookitty, Wootini, X22293x, Xanthar, Xavier86, Xavierp94, Xeworlebi, Xhead12, Xiamcitizen, Xyzzy613, Yann78, Yeeshenhao, Yoasif, Yurik, Yvolution, Yworo, Z.E.R.O., Zach.vega1, Zachlutz, Zaiken, Zak.l, Zapptastic, Zelazil, Zoffdino, Zoicon5, Zollerriia, Zomic13, ZooCrewMan, Zoombus, Zpeidar, Zzuuzz, Ævar Arnfjörð Bjarmason, 의견 정리하기, , , 1809 anonymous edits

Single-player video game *Source*: http://en.wikipedia.org/w/index.php?title=Single-player_video_game *Contributors*: 041744, Aiken drum, AI3xil, AlistairMcMillan, Angelbo, Bilbo571, Black Falcon, BluesD, Cadsuane Melaidhrin, Careydaniels, Chaos5023, Cherkash, Dadude3320, Dark Pulse, Dbiel, Deuxhero, Diego Moya, Disavian, Falcon8765, Fish and karate, FriedMilk, Gtrmp, Holek, IGeMiNix, INkubusse, JForget, JaGa, Jagged 85, Jeffrey Mall, Jezhotwells, JimmyBlackwing, K1Bond007, Kariteh, Kchishol1970, LOL, LedgendGamer, LiDaobing, Lightsup55, Marasmusine, Mauler90, Mechasheherezada, Meelar, Mitaphane, Mrwojo, Necoplay, OboeCrack, Optim, Ost316, Panser Born, Panther991, Piecemealcranky, Poetic Decay, Quoth, RAlafriz, Ras, Razorflame, Remurmur, Resound, Retodon8, Rhe br, Rigadoun, RoyBoy, S@bre, SMcCandlish, SharkD, Shrumster, Sitearm, Slike, Smurrayinchester, Snowolf, Soetermans, Sopemting, SuperMarius, Surachit, TheCatalyst31, Theblackgecko, Theresa knott, Vassilios de Veritas, Vendettax, Video game fan11, Violinmaster4321, Vishnava, Zacatecnik, 92 anonymous edits

Image Sources, Licenses and Contributors

Printed by Books on Demand GmbH, Norderstedt / Germany